KILLING TIME

KILLING TIME

The nightmare of an innocent man branded a killer

NOEL FELLOWES

A LION BOOK

Copyright © 1986, 1993 and 1996 Noel Fellowes

The author asserts the moral right
to be identified as the author of this work

Published by
Lion Publishing plc
Sandy Lane West, Oxford, England
ISBN 0 7459 3604 0
Albatross Books Pty Ltd
PO Box 320, Sutherland, NSW 2232, Australia
ISBN 0 7324 1459 8

First edition 1986
This revised edition 1996
10 9 8 7 6 5 4 3 2 1 0

A catalogue record for this book is available
from the British Library

Printed and bound in Great Britain
by Cox & Wyman Ltd, Reading

Contents

Foreword

During the 30 years I've been studying miscarriages of justice, I've found the most common cause to be over-zealousness on the part of the police.

The police light on some tiny, circumstantial piece of evidence to connect a person with the crime. Desperate to get results, they allow their suspicions to harden into certainty. Believing they are serving the best interests of justice, they then:

    a) Try to browbeat the suspect into a confession.

    b) Pressurise witnesses to say what they want them to say.

    c) Suppress or ignore other evidence that is favourable to the accused.

    d) 'Lose' documents that support the accused's alibi.

The case of Noel Fellowes is a classic case of this sort of malpractice. Arrested for the murder of a 67-year-old debt collector called Harold Parkinson, the only evidence against him was that his mother-in-law's name was found in Parkinson's debt collection book, and that someone had seen Parkinson get into a taxi on the day of the murder!

On this flimsy scenario the Lancashire CID, under

Detective Chief Superintendent Mounsey, went to work. Having grilled Noel Fellowes all night to extract a confession and failed, they then 'persuaded' various witnesses to say that he had a grudge against Parkinson (whom he had never met) and that the cravat found on Parkinson's body belonged to Fellowes (who didn't own a cravat). They suppressed evidence that pointed to others and failed to ascertain that the cravat belonged to Parkinson. In addition, the taxi company's records that would have established Noel Fellowes' alibi mysteriously went missing.

Faced with this mass of false evidence, it isn't surprising that the jury found Mr Fellowes guilty of manslaughter. Sentenced to seven years, he served four before being released on parole. One of the most heartening sections of this book is Noel Fellowes' refusal to be crushed by the prison system and how, despite recurrent nightmares and two beatings-up, he succeeded in blossoming physically and educationally.

It wasn't for another nine years, however, that, thanks to a supergrass [stool pigeon], Parkinson's real assailant was discovered. Upholding Noel Fellowes' appeal against conviction, the Lord Chief Justice had some mildly critical things to say about the conduct of the Lancashire police.

In my view that wasn't enough. What was needed wasn't just the clearing of his name, but a searching inquiry into just how an innocent man had come to be convicted. In his Christian faith the author has forgiven his transgressors. But we need to ensure that this doesn't make it easier for those who come after to become transgressors themselves.

What in the long run can be done to prevent further miscarriages of justice? In my view there's only one solution, which is to abandon the accusatorial system of justice which has been responsible for so many miscarriages in the past, and in its place to adopt a modified form of the inquisitorial or European system, in which the initial investigations into serious cases aren't conducted by policemen hungry for results, but by a supervisory, neutral legal official.

Had such officials been operating in Britain these last 30 years, a score of prisoners or ex-prisoners I could name (and some whom I have named) would never have come to trial, let alone have been convicted. Noel Fellowes is the latest, but not, I fear, the last.

Ludovic Kennedy

1 The Wrong Man

It was the afternoon of February 26, 1970. I woke feeling tired after my all-night stint at the taxi office. Nightwork seemed a gross inconvenience to my social life. Still, a cold washdown, a cup of tea and I'd be ready to face another day. The apartment I shared with a friend was in disarray, but that could wait for a cleaning blitz at the weekend.

My brain started to function at last. My stomach was telling me I was very hungry, so I decided to buy fish and chips on the way to work.

It was a typical cold, damp February day. I walked down Thornton Road towards the chip-shop. I decided to get some cigarettes as my packet showed signs of urgent crisis.

'Twenty Embassy and a *Lancashire Evening Post*, please,' I muttered to the shop assistant. Coming out of the shop I remember glancing at the paper headline: 'KILLING IN OVERTON'.

'That doesn't happen in villages like Overton, or even in Morecambe,' I thought. It was winter. No one moved in the town; everyone hibernated. Still, there's nothing like gossip and speculation to wake people up.

I strolled down Euston Road wondering what could have happened. The detail was sparse—only that a large number of detectives had been brought into the area.

When I got to the taxi office, the place was buzzing with excitement about the murder.

'Who needs all this?' I thought. I'd only surfaced a couple of hours ago and I hadn't had anything to eat. Betty told me Lynn wanted picking up from work at the hairdressers. I took my driver's log-sheets, jumped in the car and went to pick her up.

I'd met Lynn after my recent separation from my wife. My marriage had been a combination of incompatibility and reluctance on my part to accept marriage responsibilities. The emotional strain, coupled with disenchantment, had led to my recent resignation as a police constable. My job as a taxi driver gave me breathing space before deciding what direction to take. Besides, as a seaside resort, Morecambe offered little other than seasonal work.

The opportunity for a carefree romance was refreshing. It allowed me to share my innermost thoughts on the rights and wrongs of my decision to separate from my wife. I'd never tried to disguise the fact that I was going out with Lynn. I'd met her after I'd left my wife. It was a very good relationship and we seemed to complement each other.

Lynn came from a stable, secure background. Her parents welcomed me into their home. I had, of course, assured them that my involvement with their daughter wasn't a quick fling. I was very fond of her and the feeling was mutual.

After taking Lynn home, I was busy carrying passengers until about midnight. Then I headed for the office to man the phone until the day staff started at 6a.m. The conversation in the small hours was about the Overton killing. There seemed to be more police than residents and we joked about needing to watch our speed until they'd left the area.

Winter days passed slowly in the heavily-shuttered seaside town. The place was littered with police. Posters of the dead man were all over town and police trucks using loudspeakers were appealing for anyone who had known Harold Parkinson to come forward.

A breakthrough came when police revealed that they'd received an anonymous phone call from a man saying he'd seen Parkinson board a taxi on the night before he died. The police decided to interview all taxi drivers in the area. They arrived at the taxi office on 5 March and were given the names of all the drivers.

As a result, I was asked to go to the Murder HQ in Overton to answer some questions. Naturally, I agreed. I had nothing to hide.

At the Murder HQ two detectives sat me down and began routine questioning. Did I know the man? I didn't. They showed me a photo of the dead man and asked if I'd ever carried him as a passenger. To the best of my recollection, I hadn't. I told them that Parkinson's face *looked familiar*, but I couldn't be certain. Besides, our taxi business was in Morecambe, seven or eight miles from Overton. If Parkinson had wanted a taxi he'd have taken one locally.

The detectives told me that Parkinson fancied himself as a private investigator. They knew I was separated from my wife and suggested there might be some connection. I replied that I had nothing to hide—my friends and family knew my situation.

Next they said my mother-in-law's name was found in a book belonging to Parkinson and they thought he might have been employed by her to follow me. My mother-in-law was always trying to make trouble for me, I told them. I had no knowledge of her hiring anyone, but I had no contact with her. Perhaps my wife and/or mother-in-law employed him. 'Why don't you ask them?' I replied.

Again they asked if I knew Parkinson. He used to come to Morecambe Police Station with information about happenings in the town. I said that I *might* have seen him or heard talk about him while I was a policeman. And if he *were* a private detective, my wife *might* have hired him. It was all speculation.

The interview lasted half an hour and I made a statement confirming what I'd said.

That afternoon I returned to the taxi office feeling a little disturbed that my mother-in-law's name was in Parkinson's book. When I picked up

14

Lynn from work I told her about the interview. To take the intensity out of the situation I jokingly said, 'Next stop Walton Jail.' She said I shouldn't joke about things like that, but I never took anything seriously.

As I ate with Lynn and her family we discussed the murder. I threw in a few remarks like, 'I told them I didn't tie him that tight.' Little did I know that those remarks, made in jest, were to cost me years of terrible suffering.

The afternoon of March 6 I was woken by a loud banging on the door of the apartment. I stumbled into my trousers and answered the door. Two hefty six-foot men stood there.

'Noel Fellowes?' asked one.

'That's me. Who on earth are you?'

They flashed their warrant cards and walked into the apartment. They informed me that with my consent they wanted to take some of my clothes for forensic analysis. I thought they were joking. To my dismay, they weren't.

I asked why they wanted my clothes and they said it was for elimination. At that point I said the joke was going too far and I was going to consult a lawyer. The whole incident didn't make sense. But after quick consideration I told them to take what they wanted as I had nothing to hide.

After they left, a feeling of bewilderment welled up in me. I made myself a drink and sat down to think. What on earth did they want my clothes for? Did they suspect I was somehow involved in the crime? It was strange to feel so frightened by the police.

In the early evening of 8 March I was in the taxi office when two detectives entered. They said that Chief Superintendent Mounsey, in charge of the murder investigation, wanted to interview me at the Murder HQ in Overton. I agreed to go with them and they drove me to the Memorial Hall in Overton to meet Mounsey.

It was a strange journey. No one spoke. I tried to reason out why they wanted to interview me. As we arrived, I felt apprehension. I'd already told them everything I knew.

We walked through the main entrance and were met by the noise of intense human activity. Small mountains of paper were stacked on every desk with detectives sifting through them. Street maps on the wall were colour-coded with comments written on them.

I was led down the avenue of desks to a single glass door with the inscription 'Det. Sup. Mounsey' on it. I was ushered in and ordered to sit on a wooden chair.

A tall, overweight, middle-aged man walked in. With a gruff introduction of himself as Mounsey and the opening words, 'I'm not very happy about the statement you've given my officers,' the interview began.

My first response was to tell him I wasn't happy at being brought back to the Murder HQ. This incensed him and he retorted that his men had been working round the clock and he wasn't going to be messed about by an upstart who had a little knowledge of the law.

'Not the best start,' I thought. 'I'd better keep my thoughts to myself.'

Mounsey was an awesome character. He studied my earlier statement then asked about my involvement with Parkinson. I said again that I'd never met him. He went over the same grounds as before and I made the same statement I'd made earlier.

Mounsey was having none of it. He told me he'd had information from two people. Apparently, I'd told them Parkinson was following me and I'd seen him in Morecambe and beaten him up. I calmly replied that I'd never met the man.

By this time, the adrenaline was flowing as fear crept over me. The fear grew as Mounsey said things like, 'We know you did it. Why don't you get it off your chest? We know you didn't mean to kill him.'

As I continued to plead my innocence, he became more determined, shouting and banging his fist on the table. By this time fear had engulfed me and I just broke down. As hard as I tried to fight back the tears, they just kept flowing. Deep shock set in and I fought inwardly to say the words: 'I've told you over and over again. I've never met the man. I know nothing about this crime.'

'Right, lads,' Mounsey said. 'Wrap it up here. Let's go to Lancaster Police Station. We've got him.'

I broke into a cold sweat in total disbelief. Surely this was a dream? Before I could utter another word, a pair of handcuffs were snapped tightly over my wrists. I thought of the number of times I'd snap-ped handcuffs on other people. Now I had first-hand experience of the feeling—complete and utter horror.

They led me into the main hall, Mounsey proclaiming, 'We've got him. Have an early night.' Two stone-faced detectives grabbed my arms and walked me through the narrow corridor of chairs and desks.

What a contrast! An hour ago the hall was a mass of activity. Now there was a deathly stillness. The typewriters had stopped, the phones were silent. There wasn't even the sound of rustling paper. I was conscious of people staring as I passed them. Most faces were expressionless but I could hear their thoughts in unison: 'You've had it.'

We travelled to Lancaster at high speed. My whole body was shaking and nausea crept steadily over me. 'If this is how it feels when you're innocent, how do people feel when they're guilty?' I asked myself.

Surely this was a case of mistaken identity, gross incompetence or absolute lies? So many questions buzzed through my head that I couldn't catch up with them. The silence in the car was strange after those browbeating exchanges. Perhaps it was a psychological tactic—a lull before the storm.

On arrival I was escorted to an interview room. My nervous state had subsided a little and a small shield of inner confidence raised itself. Mounsey came into the room wearing a menacing expression, and the interrogation started.

We went over the same ground we'd covered before. I repeatedly told him I didn't know Parkinson and had no interest in coin collecting.

'What about the fight you had with him?'

'I never met the man,' I said.

Mounsey and the other three detectives in the room seemed to be outdoing each other by approaching the same questions from different angles. I knew it would only be a matter of time before they concluded I was telling the truth.

By now I was tired of the same old questions. I said to Mounsey I'd answered them all in total truth and I wanted to go home. He told me I wasn't going anywhere until he'd finished with me.

The tactics changed. The detectives left, including Mounsey, and a fresh team took over. When I got up to go they pushed me back down. I asked them if they were the heavy mob. One of them replied, 'You should know we don't do things like that.'

They showed me large, horrific photos of the dead man. He'd obviously been badly beaten, tied up in the most intricate fashion and gagged.

'How did he get the cuts and bruises?' they asked.

'I haven't a clue,' I replied.

'You're separated from your wife; your mother-in-law employed him to follow you; we had a phone message that he got into a taxi; and we have two witnesses who confirm that you told them he was following you and that you beat him up a few days before. Come on, make it easy on yourself. Tell us what *really* happened.'

Again I could only deny the accusations. The

strain was starting to tell on me and my mind drifted into confusion. I'd been interrogated for six hours. It was now one o'clock in the morning.

Six hours of intense questioning and still they didn't believe me. Signs of tiredness and frustration appeared in their faces and voices. They became irate. They'd gone full circle and were back to shouting accusations and desk-banging with clenched fists. This certainly raised the level of fear in me, but how can you confess to something you haven't done?

Later, Mounsey returned with another team.

'You've done well keeping us all up,' he said. 'Now tell us about the person or persons you're covering up for. There must have been more than one person who committed this crime.'

'I'm not covering up for anyone. I know absolutely nothing.'

'You're an ex-policeman and probably a clever one to have covered your tracks after killing this man. Now the game's over. At the very worst it'll only be manslaughter. Come on—tell us the truth.'

Again I denied any knowledge of the crime. I was totally fatigued, mentally and physically. They seemed hellbent on stitching me up, but why? I was a free man, living in a democratic society. Yet I'd been refused permission to leave, denied access to a telephone or contact with friends and family and—worst of all—denied a lawyer. So much for democratic rights.

I told Mounsey I felt totally shattered and wanted to go.

'Not until you've given us what we want.'

'I've told you all I know. Stop this merry-go-round. Either charge me or let me go.'

'You're going nowhere!' he shouted.

The questioning continued. We covered the same ground and I was down to single-word answers. No. No. No. At 2.30a.m. another detective came in and sheepishly whispered to Mounsey, then left.

Mounsey looked at me and said, 'Your wife's downstairs. You can see her if you want.'

What on earth was *she* here for? I hadn't seen her for a couple of months. They handcuffed me and led me down to another interview room and there was my wife, looking pale and nervous.

My opening comment was, 'What's going on? They think I had something to do with the Overton murder.'

'You must tell them the truth, Noel, and everything'll be all right.'

'I've told them the truth all along.'

She kept saying, 'Tell them the truth and they'll help you.'

At this point I realized I was a scapegoat for someone. A conspiracy was being built—and I was the victim. Now they were using my wife to break down my defences to extract a confession. I pleaded with her to phone my parents or a lawyer. She said the police had told her to tell no one. They'd look after it. How naive people are, presuming a policeman is beyond reproach and must be telling the truth always.

I pleaded with her to contact someone. But she gave no indication whether she would or wouldn't. With that, the visit ended and I was led back to the original interview room.

'Now we've let you see your wife, how about clearing up this whole mess?' asked Mounsey.

I gave the same reply: 'I know nothing.'

They started from the beginning again, asking leading and subtle questions like, 'When you hit him, you didn't mean to hit him, did you?'

I had nothing left—no strength of mind or physical energy. I felt dizzy, sick and insecure. What had started as an ordinary day had turned into a terrible nightmare. From that point on I remained totally silent and at 5.30a.m. Mounsey directed his men to lock me up and let me rest for a while.

I'd been questioned nonstop for 10 ½ hours and they'd achieved nothing more than had been gained in the first 15 minutes. Surely by now they *must* know I was telling the truth. What they'd said was only speculation and, at best, circumstantial.

They took me to the basement cell block. The constable in charge ordered me to take off my jacket and empty my pockets, then locked me up. I couldn't be bothered to protest. They could have thrown me into a rat-infested dungeon for all I cared—as long as they let me sleep.

I emerged from the depths of sleep feeling a hand shaking me vigorously. I reluctantly opened my eyes and the full horror of my predicament flooded back to me. It wasn't a figment of some devilish nightmare. It was real.

The constable said the men in the station reckoned I'd done well standing up to all the questioning. Big deal. They'd all but destroyed me and now this jerk was giving me a backhanded compliment.

He supplied me with soap and a towel, and brought me something to eat and drink. Two detectives came to take me upstairs. Strange—after all I'd endured, my mind was alert but my body was functioning with nervous disorder.

The detectives tried to get me to talk but I kept my mouth shut. I was taken to the police surgeon, a civilian doctor. He examined me, then explained that the police wanted samples of my blood, hair, nails and scrapings from beneath my nails. I broke my silence and told him I had no objection as I had nothing to hide.

I was taken for fingerprinting. It was unnecessary—all police are fingerprinted and my prints would still be on file—but they insisted. They asked more questions but I just stared at them and remained silent. Time was on my side. I knew they'd soon have to allow me legal representation or charge me. Before long they locked me up again.

My mind went into overtime as I searched my memory for clues as to why they thought it was me. The worst thing was trying to remember my movements two weeks previously from 6p.m. on Tuesday 24 February until mid-morning on Thursday 26 February. I'd been on nights and knew that my work-sheets could account for that time. The rest was pretty sketchy.

It would have been easier if I could have spoken to people, but I was isolated. I was trapped in a situation in which I didn't even understand the rules. I spent the afternoon thinking over my dilemma.

In the evening two detectives took me upstairs and showed me into a room. Chief Inspector Howson stood there, with Mounsey, and read out from a piece of paper.

'Keith Noel Fellowes, you are charged that between 24 and 26 February you murdered Harold Parkinson... You are not obliged to say anything; anything you say will be taken down and...'

My heart pounded faster and faster. My legs began to crumble with the shockwaves jerking through my body.

I looked coldly at Mounsey, eyeball to eyeball, then spoke.

'Not guilty.'

He looked at me with a fixed expression.

The exercise over, Howson told me that they would inform my lawyer. I said I didn't have one.

'Never mind,' he said. 'We'll pick one off the legal aid list for you.'

And that was it.

2 Scene of the Crime

Harold Parkinson was an old man who saw life through the eyes of a comic-strip hero. A man of 67, he was a private investigator, police informer and martial arts warrior—in his own mind. He was an old man who lived in the world of his own imagination.

There weren't many like him in Overton, its population of 831 a sedate mixture of retired, farming or professional people not given to eccentricity or play-acting. Its isolation—cut off daily at one end by the tide—was a comforting barrier to the tourists at Morecambe and the everyday business of the rest of Lancashire.

Harold John Driscoll Parkinson had lived in the terraced cottage in Overton's Main Street for seven years. He was a local man, born into a well-off family. His father ran a successful jewellery store in Morecambe and Harold Parkinson had inherited his wealth without ever having to work hard for a living. Over the years he had tried his hand at several jobs but had never really settled on anything.

It's difficult to piece together what he had done because of the embellishments he laid in later life. He said his fortune came from buying and selling coins and antiques. But the money left him by his parents set him up in a comfortable existence which he didn't need to improve on.

Parkinson was a colourful local figure. When he introduced the first Volkswagen to the village, many peered in wonder. Later, they couldn't conceal their curiosity when he bought a diesel Mercedes. One of his other habits—drinking—interrupted his free-wheeling days when he was banned from driving by the police.

Even in old age, Parkinson was active. He was out and about most days. Occasionally, local firms would contact him to do some minor debt-collecting work. His success in this role was largely a result of his being over six feet tall and well-built, with a swaggering gait that any sergeant-major would have been proud of.

Parkinson often visited the Queen's Hotel in Morecambe at lunchtime and Overton's two pubs, the Ship and the Globe, in the evening. He enjoyed heated debate and occasionally he became too disruptive and was barred from the premises. The ban would soon be lifted, though.

Retired fisherman Jimmy Braid had known Harold Parkinson since his teens.

'During the war he worked on security at Vickers Shipyards where he lost the finger off one hand. He was always vague about his associates. He often upset people with his offhanded attitude.'

Not everyone shared this view. Indeed, there was little standing room when he threw a New Year's Eve party a few weeks before his death.

The cottage in Main Street had a distinctive charm, with its stone fireplace, timber-beamed ceiling and collection of antiques. Family photos decorated a grand Welsh dresser.

Mrs Josephine Hockenhull spent four years as his home help. 'He sometimes said he could chop a man down with one blow. He'd grip my hand and I couldn't get loose. He fancied himself in Kung Fu. But I never took any notice of him. He was full of stories. Told me surgeons had put a plate in his head after a road accident.'

Parkinson was famous for his coin collection, started by his father. Over the years he collected coins from around the world. He helped form the Morecambe, Lancaster and District Numismatic Society and joined the International Coin Group. His hobby was regularly featured in local newspapers.

Word of his expertise spread—ultimately into the wrong hands. His collection of valuable coins was kept in a cabinet in a back room, but he was very security-conscious. Visitors would hear the clicking of locks and bolts the instant they left the house.

His desire to be a policeman meant that he sought out police company, yet had little of real importance to tell them. He saw himself as a private investigator who would fearlessly tackle any case. In truth, he probably never did any investigation. But this whim later had a bearing on how others were to regard him. And it had a direct effect on my life.

On Tuesday 24 February, 1970, Parkinson woke with stomach pains. When Bernard Darby, a shop proprietor, arrived to take him to the library at 9.30, he found him not well enough to travel. Mr Darby and Mrs Hockenhull made sure he was feeling better before leaving. It was the last time they saw him alive.

Both later recalled that Parkinson was expecting a phone call that day, probably to do with his coins, and Mrs Hockenhull was able to describe to the police the clothes he'd been wearing.

Three friends of Parkinson saw him the next day at different times. But a shock lay in store for Mr Darby on Thursday 26 February when he came to the cottage to pick up the old man.

'The curtains downstairs were drawn and there was no sign of him outside in the garden. There was a newspaper stuck through the letterbox and a bottle of milk nearby. The door was slightly ajar. I pushed it open and called, "Harold."

'I went into the living-room, which was generally disturbed. I then saw that the door to the understairs cupboard was open wide. I saw a bundle on the floor and realized it was a body. It had a gag round the face and a finger missing. It was Harold Parkinson.'

Two minutes after he phoned, the police arrived. Amid the tragic confusion, the phone rang. It was Elizabeth Barrett, a coin enthusiast, who'd planned to invite Parkinson for a meal. Mr Darby had to tell her he was dead.

The old man was tied in a manner later described by a barrister as 'trussed like a turkey'. The victim's ankles were pinned together by a red tie, fastened in a tight granny knot. The calves were held by a bandage fastened in the same way. Above the knees, a cable was tied in figure-of-eight fashion, immobilising the thighs. A metal-buckled webbing-strap was wrapped round the upper legs, a loose end looped round the left arm.

The wrists were clasped together at the front, right hand on top of left. A silk handkerchief was used in a figure-of-eight, the first loop tied in a granny knot, the second in a square knot. There was bandage round the hands, some of it crossing in a big X over his chest and, fatally, round his neck.

Electrical cable still connected to a vacuum cleaner was circled round his bulky frame. The lower half of his head was obscured by purple cloth which was later to assume vital importance.

It took the mortuary staff hours to untie the ligatures. Whoever had bound him had gone to a lot of trouble to stop him raising the alarm. Their precautions had proved too successful. The old man had probably struggled so much that he had tightened his bonds and strangled himself. It was clear he'd been beaten before being trussed up. A quarter of his face was covered in dry blood and there were bruises elsewhere.

Police quickly started to identify the various possibilities surrounding his death. Was it a burglary that went wrong? Did Parkinson have enemies? Could he have tied himself up in a masochistic search for kicks? For one officer, the death was a double shock. Detective Constable Jack Ellison had known Parkinson personally for six years.

Within an hour of the body's discovery, word leaked to the press. Three *Lancashire Evening Post* reporters were assigned to the story. The killing had a big impact on local newspaper front pages but was dismissed in only a few lines in the national press.

Even so, Overton had never seen anything quite like this. An invasion of police officers and reporters swarmed everywhere.

News was almost inadvertently suppressed, reported the *Evening Post*, when 'a queue of sweating reporters, clutching exclusive copy with deadlines on their minds, almost burst into tears when a telephone engineer calmly closed the kiosk and resolutely refused to rewire a light fitting'. Not everyone, it seems, was sharing the village's new-found sense of urgency.

When the copy was filed, it more often than not contained unflattering remarks about the victim—editors were safe in the fact that they couldn't libel the dead.

There were two immediate priorities for police arriving at the scene. First, scientists had to carry out an inch-by-inch study of the house. This was the job of Dr Alan Clift, chief biologist at the North Western Forensic Science Laboratory in Preston. He found bloodstains on the hearth, carpet, radio and the legs of a stool. He also took some buttons for further study.

Second, they had to decide the medical cause of Parkinson's death. Home Office pathologist Dr Brian Beeson, based at the Royal Lancaster Infirmary, made a lengthy report. One theory stood out. Death was caused by strangulation from the bandage—a pressure 'maintained for several minutes at least'.

Dr Beeson said facial bruises could have been caused by punches or 'chops'. The old man had suffered five fractured ribs and other internal injuries consistent with 'rabbit punches' or even kicks. A fracture to the lower jaw could have happened after death.

After police photographer Detective Sergeant George Brogden had taken 18 black-and-white photos in the living-room and more in colour later in the mortuary, detectives were free to examine the books, diaries and other documents.

It was obvious from the outset that this wasn't going to be an easy crime to solve. There seemed no clear motive, no immediate witnesses and no high-profile suspects. But the young detectives who streamed from many parts of the north-west of England took up the challenge.

They couldn't fail—they had Joe Mounsey.

3 Joe Mounsey:
The Means to an End

There weren't many policemen in England with a reputation like Joe Mounsey's. His tenacity, single-mindedness and shrewd interpretation of criminal psychology were legendary. There was one quality Mounsey never seemed to lack—his ability to get results.

Strangely, he started his career patrolling the same Morecambe streets that were my patch as a young constable. For three years PC Mounsey dealt with the hard-drinking holidaymakers and the shoplifters that plague every busy trading centre. After a few months in the traffic department, he was transferred to the Criminal Investigation Department. Although the Lancashire branch was the biggest in England outside London's Scotland Yard, Mounsey's initiative and total dedication began to get him noticed.

Promotion came in 1957 when Mounsey, a former Guardsman, was sent on an assignment to

Cyprus. He joined anti-terrorist officers on the trail of Nicos Sampson, wanted gunman on the island.

At 3a.m. one January, Mounsey and two other officers stormed a cottage near Nicosia and seized Sampson as he loaded his Sten gun. A burst of machine-pistol fire from one of the policemen persuaded their prisoner to come quietly. Sampson admitted 20 political killings under the late General Grivas. Years later, Sampson became president of Cyprus after a coup.

Later that year, after Mounsey had married Margaret, a former policewoman, he returned to routine work in Widnes, Lancashire. Within seven years he had become detective chief inspector and was posted to Ashton-under-Lyne. There he faced his biggest challenge—investigating the Moors Murders—as a result of which he became known to millions of people in the UK.

He had been intrigued by the dossier on 12-year-old John Kilbride, who had left a local fair just before 6p.m. on 23 November, 1963 to go home but had never made it. Mounsey visited the boy's home and came away resolving to crack the case. Soon, John Kilbride's identity was submerged in police circles. He became known as 'Mounsey's lad'.

It was a whole year before there was any hint of a breakthrough. On 6 October, 1965, teenager Edward Evans was found murdered at a house in Hattersley, near Manchester. Two people were being questioned—Ian Brady and his lover, Myra Hindley. A search of their home revealed a notebook containing the words 'John Kilbride'.

The officer-in-charge phoned Mounsey—in whose office a poster of the boy had remained for two years after the disappearance. In *Beyond Belief*, Emlyn Williams describes how Mounsey arrived to interview Brady at Stalybridge police station: 'Five minutes early, the bulldog with something between his teeth which he would never let go. He had the exact mind of a watchmaker or a miniaturist, the sort of man who can stare a jigsaw puzzle into creeping together.'

The *Police Review* summed up Mounsey's feelings during the dramatic meeting with Brady. He 'knew, as all good detectives know, that this was the man he had been looking for'.

Getting little information from Brady and Hindley, Mounsey spent hours poring over photographs from their family album. He became obsessed by two of them showing Hindley looking at a spot of moorland in front of her. Mounsey organized massive searches of the surrounding moors. He drove miles trying to place the photos with the skyline. Eventually, he settled on a remote spot. The body was found soon after. In May 1966 Brady and Hindley were both jailed for life, at Chester Assizes.

By the end of 1967, Mounsey had risen to detective chief superintendent in the Northern District Crime Squad. For the next seven years he was head of Lancashire CID, earning a British Empire Medal.

This was the calibre of the man who arrived on 26 February in tiny Overton. His task was to take charge of a homicide that seemed insignificant compared to his other cases. But Joe Mounsey was the sort who would apply the same vigilance in solving every case.

Mounsey first visited Harold Parkinson's seventeenth century cottage in Main Street. He was then off down the road to the Memorial Hall where his 'control post and enquiry organization' had been set up. He was pleased with the local response and commented: 'The degree of public co-operation here is very good indeed and we are grateful to everyone for helping our enquiries.'

Like other high-ranking officers, he knew how to deliver a carefully prepared press statement without offending anyone. He had cultivated press contacts for years. Reporters loved him. He'd shower photos like confetti whenever possible. He'd also impart off-the-record information. This ensured that it remained unpublished until Mounsey okayed it. It was crafty news management, but the journalists willingly agreed to it. He realized that the printed word would always be scrutinised more than any throwaway remark, so he took care to choose his words.

Mounsey's authoritative manner and experience set him apart from any other officer. The Murder HQ was soon packed with police, all with specific roles to play. There was a taxi squad, a house-to-house squad, a background squad and many others. They filed reports back to the control room which were analyzed by Mounsey, his superintendent and a researcher. The bosses would then underline phrases that needed following up or clarifying.

The important thing was to talk to everybody who might know something about the victim. The difficulty was this: Harold Parkinson may have been disliked by many people, but this was Overton, not Chicago. Grudges had never ended in even mild violence before. It seemed likely that robbery had been the motive. Yet it looked as if nothing had been stolen.

'Trussed Up Body: Mystery Deepens', the headlines said on 27 February. The newspaper report said that police were baffled why anybody would want to tie up and kill a 67-year-old pensioner. It also said that the victim was last seen alive at 4p.m. on Tuesday 24 February.

This is significant because the three acquaintances of Parkinson mentioned in chapter two who had seen him alive the following day were to tell Mounsey's men a different story.

Charles Ramsey, the barman from Queen's Hotel, spotted Parkinson at 1.35p.m. on 25 February walking along Queen Road in Morecambe. 'His coat was buttoned and he had his hands in his pockets.' Ramsey was sure he had the day right—Wednesday was his day off. He was also certain this was Parkinson. 'Although he was about 20 yards away from me I easily recognized him.' Ramsey had served the old man with drinks most lunchtimes for the past eight years.

Richard Luke, a bus-driver, had been driving the 8.30a.m. to Euston Road bus station when he saw Parkinson twice. The second time, 'he lifted his hand to me in acknowledgement—I have no doubt it was Harold'.

Just as convinced about time was Jimmy Braid, a retired fisherman: 'I last saw him about 10.30a.m. on Wednesday the 25th when I went to a small shed situated next to the air-raid shelter where I kept my car, at the rear of Parkinson's house. I got some bolts out of the shed and as I was walking back I saw Parkinson and he asked me if I was going to Morecambe.'

Three different sightings, all on the 25th. Lack of hard evidence meant Mounsey was coy with announcements. It was Saturday before he declared that the coin dealer had been strangled. But he refused to go one step further and confirm it was murder.

Police also revealed that the old man was understood to have had a phone call about his coin collection at 9p.m. on Wednesday. They didn't name their source, but it must have been Lancaster telephone exchange operator Mrs Sylvia Kinnaird. Her observations were eventually deemed irrelevant by the police, but they certainly would have been a boost for me!

However, Mounsey developed the importance of this phone call once more before it was ditched. The *Lancashire Evening Post*, 2 March: 'The Overton death riddle is now centring on Mr X—the man who phoned wealthy coin collector Harold Parkinson and arranged to meet him on the night he died. Mr Mounsey said: "The identity of this man is very important. I feel that he is a key figure in our investigation." '

There was no feedback on this, so it was back to the hard slog of routine interviews, poster distribution and loudspeaker appeals. Detectives in the Memorial Hall were snowed under with the information, all of which needed microscopic attention.

The men on the ground were thorough. Mrs Hockenhull, the cleaner, helped with aspects of the victim's character and identified belongings later used as exhibits in court. She said: 'They never left my doorstep. I told them the last time I'd seen him alive on the 24th he'd been wearing grey flannels [trousers], a check shirt, an old tweed jacket with a tear near the sleeve, a yellow cravat and a grey pullover. That was different to what he was wearing when he was found dead.'

Her memory and attention to detail were of enormous help to the police. At the centre of the police enquiry was a purple strip of material, used as a gag, round the lower part of Parkinson's face. Mrs Hockenhull was later to make an important pronouncement about this cloth. It's not clear whether she made the same remark in 1970.

An estimated 800 statements were taken over several weeks. Because of the New Year's Eve party at the cottage, many villagers had to give fingerprints for elimination. This involvement of the community resulted in rumours and scare stories. Overton's last major criminal act, the papers said, was when William the Conqueror wrested the place from the Earl of Tostig. This murder began to resemble an Agatha Christie-style whodunnit.

Not everyone was impressed by the police operation. Businessman Rex Calverley told police about two suspicious young men in the Ship Hotel pub. 'In a village like this in the middle of winter strangers stand out. We were regulars and the pub was always very quiet at that time of year. But the police just didn't seem to follow up what we had to say.'

One of Lancashire's own officers had something to offer. PC Alan Knowles had taken a phone call at 1.22a.m. on the night in question. An anonymous caller reported an accident at the house next to Parkinson's. PC Joseph Howarth was unable to find anything on arrival and the call was put down as a prank. The value of that call was played down for reasons that didn't become obvious for more than a decade.

All this information was being processed by policemen fast becoming experts in the life of Harold Parkinson. They knew he was blood group A, as the first results started coming in from Dr Clift, the forensic scientist.

Dr Clift confirmed that 'considerable violence' had been used to break down the pensioner's resistance before he had been trussed up. Several buttons had been found on the carpet and floor, some obviously having come from the killer.

The pathologist's postmortem gave police some leeway over timing. Dr Brian Beeson put the time of death between 7a.m. and midnight on 25 February, but it could have been as early as the evening of the

24th. The strangulating tightness of the bandage, applied for several minutes, had prevented proper blood supply to the brain. The fatal vice-like grip had been an indirect result of pressure put on a lower webbing strap. This perhaps was proof that the intruder might not have intended to murder his victim. Parkinson may have brought about his own death by struggling so much that he tightened the bonds himself.

It could also prove that the intruder hadn't cared whether Parkinson lived or died. Parkinson had been punched or kicked in the face while he still had his glasses on. His chest injuries were consistent with his being 'stamped upon'.

Dr Beeson also killed off the rumour that Parkinson would have been powerless in a fist fight and unable to free himself from the ligatures because he had no little finger on his left hand and the right little finger was naturally deformed. Dr Beeson concluded that this would not significantly have impaired the function of the hands and remaining fingers.

The officers looking into Parkinson's background were told of his boasts about being a private investigator. But they were never told to turn up a single case he'd been involved in. Detective Constable Ellison, who'd known him since 1964, never mentioned it in his statement. Detective Sergeant Harold Bentham, who had met him occasionally over nine years, was more specific. 'The deceased was known locally as a private investigator but he was in fact a freelance debt-collector.'

Some of his colleagues were to close their eyes to this information.

6 March, 1970. The newspapers no longer mentioned a grey car seen outside Parkinson's house containing two men. Instead, it was another phone call that assumed elevated importance.

'An anonymous telephone call to police investigating the Overton death riddle could provide a vital clue,' trumpeted the *Lancashire Evening Post.*

'The caller who rang Morecambe police station late on Wednesday night has given detectives a lead because he appears to have been one of the last people to see Harold Parkinson alive. The man who made the call said he had seen Mr Parkinson getting into a taxi outside the GPO building in Morecambe on Wednesday 25 February at 7.40p.m.'

'It's very important that any taxi driver who may have picked up a fare corresponding to Mr Parkinson's description should contact us as soon as possible,' said Mounsey.

Two interesting points come out of this press notice. First, it indicates that police were still open-minded on whether Parkinson was alive on the Wednesday. Second, the hunt switches to find a taxi driver.

At last—a firm lead. The order echoed around the Memorial Hall as detectives attended the daily conference: *Find that driver.*

It wasn't long before two threads of the enquiry fused together. And there was a name that Mounsey could target: Keith Noel Fellowes.

The first tenuous link to put me under suspicion was that I drove a cab for Charlie & Kim's taxi firm in Euston Road, Morecambe. A big lad who never made the grade in the police, they said. Marriage on the rocks, maybe a playboy with his looks and tall physique.

There was excitement when they found another name in Parkinson's receipt book—Mrs Castagnini, my mother-in-law. 'What if she'd hired old Parky as a private investigator to get grounds for divorce?' one officer wondered.

Mounsey promptly had me interviewed, while other officers made subtle enquiries about my background and alibis. Those enquiries would eventually throw a 22-year-old carefree individual into Britain's waste disposal system.

Only three days after the police press release, on 9 March, 1970, I was in Lancaster Police Station, charged with the murder of Harold Parkinson.

4 The Nightmare Begins

I'd been charged with a murder I knew nothing about. I stood silent as Mounsey ordered the offi-cers to return me to my cell. My legs were like jelly and my stomach seemed to disappear. All I could think of was that *they'd actually charged me with murder*.

Before I was charged, the detectives had tried to win my confidence to obtain an admission of guilt. Now the whole atmosphere changed. There was hostility towards me. They marched me through the long corridor, down the stairs and shut me up in the cell again.

As they left, one officer said, 'You might as well get used to it. When we're through with you, it'll be life imprisonment.'

In that one line I'd been tried, convicted and sentenced. I was speechless with shock. I lay on the bed and looked around me—the cell was a mass of concrete and steel with a feeling of death about it. My whole body seemed paralyzed. My breathing became erratic and then I must have passed out.

Some while later I came to, realizing with surprise that I was still alive.

The sergeant came with a dinner tray, opened the cell door, placed the food on the floor and locked up again without a word. The last thing I wanted was to eat. Anger welled up in me. I felt like screaming or smashing hell out of the cell. Then I decided that was one of the things they'd like me to do, to show them how violent I was.

It was a real fight to keep those desires locked in. My whole being was screaming for revenge at what I'd endured in the past 24 hours. I'd been angry many times before, but never at this level. Finally, I beat the anger into submission and decided to get my head down. Tomorrow had to be a better day.

I awoke to the sound of a squeaking door. A young policeman said, 'Breakfast, Fellowes. Time to get up. You've got a busy day ahead.'

I had no desire to eat. I drank the mug of tea and prepared for the day ahead—a day over which I had no control.

Around nine, after I'd washed under police supervision, they led me to an interview room where I met Mr McHugh, who was to be my lawyer. The officers left.

McHugh looked nervous, then smiled. 'Don't worry. I'm sure we'll be able to sort this out.'

The smile was both genuine and reassuring. At last I had someone to talk to. McHugh was a small, round-faced man in his late fifties or early sixties, with striking grey hair and a warm, inviting voice. He was well dressed. He explained that the police had asked him to act in my defence and he'd be pleased to do so if I agreed. If not, I could appoint a lawyer of my choice.

I agreed to let him represent me. I didn't know any other lawyers and had never had dealings with them. In retrospect, the events leading up to this moment had been bizarre. Since my arrest I hadn't had any chance to contact anyone. It had been done by other people. Now I was confronted by someone the system had chosen for me.

The most disturbing point was that I didn't know the man's track record. All I had to go on were first impressions. But at least he was human. There was a long silence, then I fired a barrage of questions at him.

'What have the police told you? Has any of my family contacted you? Have you any idea what they're trying to do to me in here?' And so on.

He systematically answered my questions, never varying the tone of his voice. The answer to most questions was 'No', which did my morale no good. Eventually he told me I was to appear before magistrates at South Lonsdale Magistrates' Court later that day. Police were probably going to ask for a remand in police custody.

'What about application for bail?' I asked.

He doubted that it would be granted because of the serious charge.

He was right but it was difficult for me to understand. All I could think of was my innocence.

People didn't seem interested in that.

My nerves were on edge and I reached for another of the cigarettes McHugh had brought. My thinking was incoherent, my body was out of control and I was puffing continuously on cigarettes. The press notice probably said a man was helping police with their enquiries. The truth was that I was being mentally and emotionally *tortured*.

I told McHugh, 'It all seems like a nightmare that won't leave me.'

He said he could appreciate how I was feeling and in fact I was standing up to it very well.

I thought, 'You try being inside me for a while, then you'll *really* understand.'

McHugh asked me to tell him all that had happened since my arrest, which I did. He then asked if I'd ever met the deceased or had any involvement in the crime. I told him of the statement I'd made on 5 March, 1970, and of the interview when the police implied that Parkinson had been hired to follow me. I told him I'd had no involvement in the crime, so they couldn't possibly have any evidence to substantiate the charge.

McHugh replied, 'Mr Fellowes, the police couldn't have charged you if they had no evidence. Are you sure you've told me everything?'

'Of course I'm sure. Whose side are you on?'

I don't think he was convinced. He looked puzzled. But he said he'd put the wheels of defence into motion. I signed for legal aid and he left to start work on the case. I was taken back to my cell.

Lunch was served. I eagerly tucked in. What the

hell? There was no point in starving to death. My body was in a bad enough state as it was.

In the early afternoon, three detectives came and informed me that I was going to the magistrates' court.

'What about my clothes? All I have are the rags you've given me.'

'Your clothing's been sent to the forensic lab,' they said.

'Can't you get my other clothes from my apartment?'

'We've already collected them and sent them with the rest to forensic.'

'I refuse to go to court looking like this. Besides, I haven't got any socks or shoes.'

With that they grabbed my arms and a struggle took place. They never hit me, just overpowered and handcuffed me. There's not a lot you can do when three 200-pound men decide to take you.

I couldn't believe they'd take me to court dressed like that. It was degradation in its worst form. They dragged me outside, put me in the police truck and we sped off for Lancaster Castle.

My heart was thumping again and I began to shake uncontrollably. The vehicle halted and the back doors opened, revealing a glimmer of winter sunshine. It was cold and the clouds looked down in anger.

We'd arrived at the side entrance. I was offered a blanket to cover my head. I refused, saying that I had nothing to hide or to be ashamed of. I told them *they* were the ones with blankets over their heads—-blinding them to the truth. Perhaps they'd be better off removing theirs.

What a spectacle I must have looked—no socks or shoes, trousers with a 40-inch waist (mine was 32) and a shirt that would have suited a coalman! They frogmarched me up the steps to the court and into the dock. The court was empty, then I realized that they'd arranged a special court sitting to fit me in.

The magistrates entered and sat down. The police prosecutor presented his case, asking for a remand in police custody. McHugh stood up, offered no objection to the request and sat down again. I couldn't believe it. There I was, in scruffy clothes, with nothing on my feet and nobody took any notice.

I was the person being talked about. Surely magistrates could rebuke the police for bringing a prisoner before them in this manner? What about human rights? What about judges' rules? Anger was erupting again deep in the pit of my stomach. I protested at the humiliation of being brought before the court in this way. It was a waste of time. They merely approved the custody order. The whole proceedings had taken less than three minutes.

It was disturbing to witness first-hand the power the judiciary have over a person who at the very best has only been charged. 'Innocent until proven guilty' is a flag of convenience the judiciary sails under. At police college we'd been taught how to treat prisoners. We were guardians of the law and employed to uphold it. The crazy thing is, I actually believed it and tried to uphold it in my short encounter with the criminal element.

Perhaps mine was an isolated case because I hadn't co-operated in their mind-games of chess. Was this a new form of psychology to degrade me and bring me to mental collapse so I'd confess?

Down the steps they dragged me, as I'd refused to walk barefoot in the wintry conditions. I was put in the truck and off we went back to the police station. Nobody said a word to me.

It had been totally unreal in the court. Everyone had seemed embarrassed at my outburst, yet no one thought of my position. The first doubts started to form. If this was what happened in front of the magistrates, what would happen at the full trial? Still, I'd have plenty of opportunity to sort that out when I saw my lawyer again.

We arrived at the police station and I was returned to my cell. In the late afternoon a senior police officer came and told me he was sorry for the way I'd been taken to court and as soon as he could he'd find me proper clothes. I was taken upstairs by two officers and introduced to another civilian police surgeon. The police would like certain samples to send away for forensic tests. He explained that I didn't have to give the samples, but they could apply for a court order to get them.

I thought for a minute and decided, 'I've got nothing to hide. They can have whatever they want.'

He began by taking a sample of blood, then a snip of my hair, nail scrapings and a scraping of my skin. The doctor asked me to undress so he could check for cuts or bruises. I said there was no need as the police hadn't beaten or injured me physically. They'd done a far better job mentally.

'It's not for that reason,' he said. 'It's to check if you've got any injuries that might show you've been in a fight recently.'

I didn't have any as I hadn't been in a fight for a number of years. Having finished, the doctor thanked me for my co-operation and departed. I went back to the cell, thoughtfully pondering the doctor and his samples.

It dawned on me that there'd been something missing. The doctor had been meticulous in his manner and examination, but at no time had he asked me if I was feeling OK or if there was anything he could do for me. I'd been charged with murder, interrogated for 12 hours, dragged to court in the middle of winter barefoot. And he hadn't even offered me an aspirin for a headache or a pill to give me better sleep.

The whole world was turning its back on me—or so it seemed.

Was I oversensitive or was I now in the early stages of paranoia? The only consolation was that it was really happening. It was no delusion of the mind or fiendish nightmare. I was imprisoned in every sense of the word—mind and body.

I began to be more rational, with a strong instinct to survive. It was time to take full stock and plan a new counterattack. I knew for certain there was no real primary evidence—documentary or forensic—as I was innocent. Their only evidence was circumstantial—the name in the notebook, flippant remarks I'd made to friends.

I began to feel better. Even the samples they'd taken would help to strengthen my case of wrongful arrest.

Then I contemplated the worst. What if they already knew they'd made a gross mistake but had decided to stitch me up? Surely they couldn't get away with it? I lay back on my bed, my mind racing from one thought to another. I wasn't reaching any single conclusion, just trying to understand how it all happened and how I managed to get into this position.

The only thread of reality was that I knew I was innocent. That was my strength, my purpose for fighting on. No one could rob me of that. My biggest problem was that I couldn't speak to anyone outside who could prove my innocence. I was on the inside looking out; no one was on the outside looking in.

The cell was becoming familiar, as though I'd lived there for some time. Yet it had barely been three days—the worst three days of my life. It seemed I'd been locked away for months.

I tried to rest for a while, only to be woken by a policeman who said I had visitors. I raised myself from my bed and looked through the steel bars to see my mother and dad entering the cell block. I decided to be brave and hold myself together. It'd make it easier for them. But when I saw them I just broke into uncontrollable crying, like a child. It was a total release of all the hurt and anguish I'd stored up over the past three days.

After some time I managed to look my parents in the face. They had tears in their eyes and I could see the inner struggle of holding the emotions back. They both seemed ashen and tired.

At first we looked at each other, expressing the hurt through our eyes. My mother stretched a comforting hand onto mine. At last, contact had been made with my family. The police were present but that didn't matter. This was a precious moment to me. It wouldn't have mattered if the whole world looked on.

'They've charged me with murder and I'm totally innocent,' I said.

'We know, son,' my father replied. 'We're here now. Don't worry, son. I'll take care of things.'

My mother echoed my father's assurance. It was good to see them. They'd travelled all the way from Bracknell in Berkshire as soon as they'd learned of my arrest. The first they knew of it was a phone call, but no details were given. I could see the shock-waves in their faces and voices.

It was strange talking to people you loved through steel bars with police listening to your every word. There was obviously much they wanted to ask but didn't. There were silences, then an attempt to strike up conversation about other matters. That failed absolutely and I asked my dad to contact my lawyer, who would be able to tell him what the present situation was.

After that, the policeman told them their time

was up and they left. My mother kept looking back, tears flowing, and my dad wrapped his comforting arm around her shoulder. The precious opportunity to talk had gone. There seemed to be so much I hadn't said to them.

I slumped on my bed trying to understand how they must be feeling. My suffering and torment had extended to my family. I felt dejected when I thought about that day. Everything was going against me. There was no light in the torture chamber of my mind. Indeed, the visit had exhausted me. My emotional defences had been opened and I felt totally drained.

I momentarily considered what was happening in the world out there. Everyone was probably moaning about the weather or arguing over which TV programme to watch, and here I was in this lockup.

My mind refused to rest and I spent a long time trying to get to sleep. At some point I must have dropped off as I was awakened again by the cell door being opened and the duty policeman serving breakfast. I eagerly ate a good helping of eggs, bacon, beans and toast, and finished with a large mug of tea. That over, it was time for the supervised washing and shaving procedure.

Mid-morning McHugh came to see me and I challenged him at not commenting on my appearing before the magistrates without socks, shoes or my own clothes. He seemed disturbed about the incident, then said he hadn't noticed my state until I'd mentioned it. By that time it was too late as the police were hurrying me out of the court. He'd made representations to the senior police officer and was sure I'd have proper clothing for my next court appearance. We then got down to more serious matters.

The legal aid forms had been sent off and he was trying to check my movements from Tuesday 24 February to Thursday 26 February, 1970. Parkinson had last been seen alive on the Tuesday afternoon and was found dead on the Thursday morning. I had difficulty remembering everything between those dates but I knew the taxi records would show my movements, and Lynn would be able to fill in the gaps.

McHugh had hired a firm of private investigators to substantiate my movements and prove my innocence. At last, things were moving in the right direction. At least there were people out there asking questions and actively working on my behalf.

Then he dropped the bombshell.

Two men who worked at the Beach Club in Heysham—Mr Thornton and Mr Bamborough—had made statements to the police. According to them, I'd told them that Parkinson had been following me and that I'd beaten him up in Morecambe around the time of the death. I just sat there dumbfounded.

'Did you beat him up, Noel?'

'I've never met Parkinson in my life.'

'Why'd these men make the statements?'

I thought for a while. 'I think the police must be kidding you, Mr McHugh, because they're nothing but lies. I made a few jokes about being interviewed by the police, but never anything like that.'

He assured me that the police were serious—the statements were one of the main reasons for my arrest. I confirmed that I'd never said such things.

'What else have the police given you?' I enquired.

'That's about all—except that your mother-in-law's name was found in Parkinson's diary. They must have come up with something more substantial to hold you. It seems to me they haven't got a case.'

'They can't possibly come up with anything, Mr McHugh. I didn't do it and I haven't any idea who did.'

'Well, we'll establish your defence as quickly as we can and try to get you out.'

With that McHugh departed.

Back in my cell I thought about what I'd just heard. What was behind the statements of Carey Thornton and John Bamborough? I knew them. I'd often taken them to work at the Beach Club and sometimes home again in the early hours of the morning. I couldn't remember doing anything against them. Why were they trying to implicate me in the murder?

I recalled a possible answer. Carey Thornton was the club manager and after dropping him off I'd go into the club for a quick drink. Several times I'd seen plain-clothes detectives drinking there and they knew I'd left the police. Maybe they'd questioned Thornton and Bamborough about me. The police may have had some hold over them or been trying to make a name for themselves. Either way I was the victim.

Looking on the bright side, I'd soon be out. Then I'd find out what *really* happened.

The police had stopped questioning me because since seeing my lawyer I'd decided to keep quiet. A couple of detectives came down several times and tried to get me to talk, but I completely ignored them.

My parents returned and we chatted quite openly. They brought me some clean clothes. My father had spoken to McHugh and they were going to keep in close contact.

Both my parents looked better since their last visit. It must have been heartbreaking for them driving home 250 miles away, knowing their son had been charged with murder.

What an agonizing journey, trying to think of a way to tell my younger brothers and sister! My elder sisters, Brenda and Carol, were married and had families. It'd perhaps be easier to break the news to them.

Two more days crept slowly by without any visits or communication from anyone. Then I was taken to the magistrates' court. This time I had proper clothes, socks and shoes.

The court went through its usual formalities. Then I was told I was to be sent to Risley Remand Centre. Shock enveloped me and the familiar feeling of fear rose inside me.

Why were they sending me to Risley? Hadn't I been through enough? Or were they set on trying to destroy me?

5 On Remand

The thought of Risley Remand Centre sent a shiver down my spine. Not long ago I'd escorted prisoners to Risley. The thought of me being there had never entered my head.

We left the court and drove back to the police station. Within minutes McHugh arrived and I was in the interview room. He assured me that his enquiries were progressing and that I wouldn't be in Risley long.

I felt sickened as I imagined what life would be like there. After all, I was an ex-policeman. Utterly dejected, I told McHugh to get me out as soon as possible.

Alone in my cell I considered my position. Things were going from bad to worse. I drifted into a depressive state. I had no mental strength left. Tears slowly ran down my face, tears of immense fear.

There was no one to talk to. The system had me totally incarcerated. The police controlled everything—when I washed, ate and slept, who I saw, the length of the visit. I wasn't ever asked to make a decision. Everything I asked for was rejected.

The police came to escort me to Risley. The journey in the back of the Ford Transit was uncomfortable. It was cold and, being handcuffed, I had difficulty keeping my circulation going. The handcuffs were so tight it was painful to move my hands. I complained, but the police just shrugged and said I shouldn't have such fat wrists.

It was a long, tiresome journey of 70 miles. But at least I was breathing fresh air again. It was obvious the two men were disgusted at escorting an ex-cop. In their eyes I was undeniably guilty.

The Transit stopped and I heard large gates being opened. My heart thumped louder. We'd arrived.

We drove a little further and halted. I was escorted to reception where the police handed over a piece of paper, saying, 'One ex-cop for you to sign for and look after.'

Everything seemed to stop, eyes coldly staring at me. A number of prisoners were cleaning up. With their gaze fixed on me, the prison officer signed the receipt and I was under their care. It's amazing that one day you're a person in a free democracy, yet at any moment you can lose the lot on the premise that you *may* have committed a serious crime. While the charge remains unproven, you can lose everything you've ever held dear.

The handcuffs were taken off, allowing the blood to flow again and revealing bruising to both wrists. Then I was ordered to be locked up until I could be processed. I was taken to a long line of cubicles and locked in one. It was similar to a changing cubicle at a swimming pool. There was a wooden bench and a small light in the ceiling.

It was enough to give anyone claustrophobia. I noticed holes had been drilled in the door for ventilation. I could imagine people wrapping their lips over the holes and drawing in great gulps of air. I sat rubbing my wrists. My fingers looked white and bloodless.

'Hey, Fellowes,' a voice whispered through the holes in the door.

'Yeah.'

'When the screws aren't looking, we're going to get you.'

Why did they want *me*? I hadn't harmed them. Then it struck me. They knew I was an ex-cop. While the police had treated me badly, the people in here didn't have any rules to restrain them. Maybe they were just trying to frighten me. Surely the prison officers would protect me?

Two hours passed and I was taken to a room where a senior prison officer sat behind a desk. He asked questions and filled in a form. He then told me the procedure for remanded prisoners. My brain couldn't take in such information—it was locked on red alert. He told me to strip as they were going to supply me with new clothes.

I stripped to my underwear, but he told me to take that off, which I did. It was degrading standing before the prison officers stripped of my pride, dignity and name. He informed me that from that moment on I was 811168 Fellowes. My forenames were redundant. Now I was a number, not a name. What more could the system do to me?

My nakedness revealed a great insecurity as I was exposed to the sniggers of my audience. Eventually I was thrown a towel and told I was to have a bath before my medical examination. I was led to the bath parlour and told I had five minutes to bathe and get dry. A trustee prisoner handed me a bar of white soap with HM Government Property engraved on it. The water had already been run into the bath and I was about to get in.

Without warning I felt a heavy blow to my head, then one to my body. As I keeled over, more and more blows raged on me. I managed to scream for help. Immediately, the blows ceased and I was left crumpled on the floor. Excruciating pain engulfed my head and the upper part of my body. A deep feeling of nausea crept through me. I realized I'd been beaten up.

'What happened, Fellowes?' an unfamiliar voice demanded. Through the barrier of my protective arms I saw a prison officer.

'Come on, lad. Tell me what happened. Did you slip off the bath?'

Dazed, I looked at him in disbelief. Surely it was obvious what had happened? I tried to pull myself up but it was useless. Within seconds, other officers lifted me to my feet, sat me on the edge of the bath and asked what had happened.

'I don't know.'

'You'd better get in the bath, then. The doctor's waiting to examine you. I'll leave one of my officers with you.'

I slumped into the tepid water, half-dazed and aching. I scanned my body for signs of cuts or blood and thankfully found no traces. Whoever had done it was expert at hitting in the right places. The officer looking on only added to my security. A few minutes ago I'd despised them for humiliating me; now they represented protection.

It was remarkable how quickly my body recovered, as if to prepare me to face the stark reality of my new environment.

After my bath the officer led me out and I noticed the two trusties mopping the floor, at the same time looking at me with expressions of pleasure. They'd been my assailants—it was written on their faces. Back in reception I was ushered into another room and confronted by a doctor. He examined me and scribbled notes down. After the examination he asked the officer about the bruises on my head and body. The officer said there'd been an accident in the bath area. The doctor asked me the same question.

'I was attacked.'

'Sir!' the officer shouted. 'You call everyone in this establishment "sir".'

The doctor gave the officer a long, hard look. 'There's too many accidents in the bath parlour. It's time someone supervised that area.'

He turned his attention to me and said that due to the seriousness of the charge I'd be allocated to the hospital wing for observation, medical reports and, not least, my protection.

The last phrase echoed in my ears—protection, what a word!

I was taken to the clothing stores to be fitted out for my stay in Risley. Two inmates (prisoners) were behind the serving hatch. They looked me up and down, then produced trousers, jacket, shirt, socks, shoes, pyjamas, underclothes and toothbrush. The uniform was brown and the shirt was a starched blue-and-white striped cotton.

'Try them on, mate.'

Everything was too big.

'None of it fits,' I said.

'Looks all right to me,' the inmate said.

'Come on, Fellowes. Let's get you to the hospital wing,' said the officer. I decided not to argue the point over clothing. We arrived at the hospital wing, where I was allocated a single cell and locked up.

It resembled the police cell I'd recently left, though it was larger with a window at the back, giving a panoramic view of the exercise yard. The yard was overlooked by cell blocks on all sides. I had a bed, chair, small table, wash bowl, water jug, small plastic jerry to use as a toilet and a booklet on prison rules.

The window was a mass of bars. It certainly didn't give the impression of being a hospital. It was a comfort that the door was locked and could only be opened by a staff member.

The clothes were dirty and ill-fitting, with the exception of the underwear. The shoes were so tight they crippled my toes, and carried the smell of the previous owner. I hoped that when I'd settled in I'd be able to make representations about my treatment so far. In the space of a few hours I'd been degraded, humiliated, beaten up and put in isolation for my own protection.

I lay on my bed, still hurting from the beating. My head was sore and aching; my ears still rang from the heavy blows they'd taken. Was there no escape from the avalanche of abuse rained on me since my arrest? Would I see life again outside the four walls of a cell?

Imagine your worst nightmare. Mine was actually taking place.

There was a jingling of keys, then in walked a prison officer, accompanied by an inmate carrying a metal tray.

'There's your dinner, Fellowes. Eat it up, lad.'

I looked at the steaming dinner. At best it looked repulsive, besides which my stomach showed no desire for food. I took one sip of the tea and instantly spat it out. Someone had laced it with salt.

It had been a long, gruelling and painful day. In utter despair and total fatigue, I crawled into bed. My mind switched off and I drifted into the protection of sleep.

The next morning I was awakened by the cell door being opened and a prison officer instructing me to slop out. I said I didn't know what he was talking about.

'Empty your jerry,' he said.

As I had not drunk anything, mine was empty, so he promptly shut the door. My injuries were now apparent. My head, chest and upper back were bruised and painful. Again the door opened and an officer instructed me to go for breakfast, so I followed the other inmates.

There was a line where other inmates were dishing out breakfast under the supervision of prison officers. My turn came and I picked up the metal tray with compartments for food. I was served porridge, bread, margarine and a mixture of corned beef with potato. I was allocated a plastic knife, fork and spoon, together with a plastic mug into which I poured tea.

Returning to my cell I was aware of inmates whispering about my previous employment. I quickened my steps and breathed a sigh of relief as I returned unharmed to the safety of the cell.

The food was appalling. My stomach heaved with every mouthful. At least the tea hadn't been laced this time.

After breakfast I lay on the bed considering the day ahead. The door opened and a prison officer angrily told me that beds were for sleeping on at night, not in the daytime. I wasn't to lie on my bed between early morning call and lights out. If I was caught in the future, I'd be put on governor's report.

I explained that this was my first day and that no one had told me the dos and don'ts.

'It's all in the prisoners' rule book, so you'd better read it.' With that he gave me a razor, brush and shaving stick and instructed me to shave.

'What sort of place is this?' I thought. There wasn't any consideration of my ignorance about rules. I was horrified at the prospect of spending time in their custody.

I had my first ever shave without hot water. It was a cutting experience in the true sense of the word. The hallmarks were there to be seen—small lacerations of the face. Coupled with the other injuries, I looked a sorry sight. They returned for the razor and I made the bed and sat on the chair. I decided to read the prison rules.

The rules were in typical civil servant language—precise and off-putting. Nowhere did I find the rule about lying on the bed. Obviously they'd made up their own local rules. The key to survival was to learn fast, otherwise the system would destroy me. I thought for a moment about those prisoners I'd brought here. I'd never considered their plight—just handed them over and left. Here I was gaining first-hand knowledge of the other side of the fence.

A small flap in the door opened and an inmate peered in.

'Hey, Fellowes, come over here.'

I nervously approached the door.

'Don't be scared. I just want to help you.'

He asked if I had any snout.

'What?'

'Cigarettes, tobacco. You know.'

'Oh, yes.' I produced my cigarettes for him.

He took a couple and said, 'If you want to live, you'd better learn about this place.' He went on to tell me the prison jargon. Officers were screws, inmates were cons, people who'd done time before were old lags. It was an education. He was on his eighth sentence and had another five months to serve.

It was my first contact with a con who seemed human. I offered him the rest of the cigarettes, but he refused saying that wasn't why he was talking to me. He wanted me to understand the system so I could protect myself. He and the other cons knew I was an ex-cop.

'Don't let them know you're frightened or they'll make your life hell,' he said. 'And don't speak to the screws or else the cons'll think you're one of them.'

I heard footsteps in the corridor. He picked up his mop and pail, closed the hatch and carried on cleaning the floor. I felt excited at the prospect of someone showing me the ropes. Now at least I could speak like them. I determined to ignore the screws, even if they tried talking with me.

Mid-morning I noticed what seemed to be hundreds of cons in the exercise yard, four or five abreast, walking round the concrete path. My door was opened and I was asked if I wanted to go out for exercise. The sheer number of cons outside convinced me that I'd be the worse for wear if I joined them. I declined.

I could hear the sound of trudging feet and voices in conversation. Soon the noise diminished and the cons vanished back to their cells. I sat thinking. I'd been locked up for a long time and no one outside seemed to know what I was going through. Maybe if they had, they'd be more active in getting me released.

The day drifted slowly by. Lunch was followed by another chance to exercise, which I again declined. Dinner came in the late afternoon and resulted in severe indigestion. My system hadn't come to terms with prison cuisine. I was visited by the medical officer, who briefly asked about my health and welfare. He said that at some stage he'd examine me in more detail. For now I'd be under observation.

At lights out—about nine o'clock—I lay thoughtfully in bed. It had been a boring day with nothing to do but kill time.

Day after day the same monotonous routine continued. The only respite was the con who shared more of his jargon and experience of prison life with me.

At least I was learning to live in prison. The food was still lousy. For the first time I was experiencing the peril of using a chamber pot six inches off the ground. It was degrading and difficult to function properly. To add to the insult, the toilet paper was coarse and sharp, with HM *Government Property* on every sheet. I doubted that anyone in prison had ever thought of stealing *that*!

The following week I was taken back to reception, given my own clothes and banged up in a sweat-box. The police arrived, handcuffed me and off we sped to Lancaster Magistrates' Court. Again there was just their small talk and my silence. Unlike my last trip, at least the handcuffs were tolerable this time.

Within a minute I was back in the vehicle, having been remanded for a further week. All the expense of a 70-mile journey for a one-minute hearing! We stopped at Lancaster Police Station to change escort and for me to see my lawyer.

McHugh looked cheerful but told me there was nothing new. Everyone they tried to interview had already been interviewed by the police.

'What about the taxi records?'

His cheerfulness disappeared. 'The police have been to the taxi office and your records for the relevant times are missing.'

I couldn't believe it. 'Surely someone knows where they are?'

He looked serious. 'The police say you got rid of them to cover your movements. Did you?'

I told him I hadn't and reminded him of my absolute innocence. He accepted my word. When I told him of the treatment I'd received at Risley, he said he'd look into the matter with the authorities. I doubted if this would achieve much. I explained that I felt totally isolated at Risley, 70 miles from friends and family and, worse, from contact with him. I wanted to be kept informed daily. He explained that there was no remand centre any nearer and that he'd see me each week when I was brought back to court.

The conversation left me dejected—nobody seemed willing to fight against the injustice I was suffering. Every ear was tightly shut to my cries for help.

As we travelled back, I felt depressed about

people's lack of concern and the missing records. Someone was trying to help me—or implicate me—in the killing. But why? All I knew was that I hadn't taken or tampered with them.

Back at Risley I was locked in the sweat-box for an hour and then reallocated to the hospital wing. I changed into the secondhand uniform. The clothes fitted far better this time. The screws escorted me back. Then came the shock.

We passed my cell, then went to the first landing where I saw a ward full of remanded cons. Fear welled up. Surely they weren't putting me here? They were.

'One on, sir,' the escort screw said to the other. My body trembled as I looked at the twenty others in the ward. The screw in charge of the ward pointed out my bed and storage cubicle and told me to put my things away. I nervously unpacked. Then I sat by the bed and one of the other cons wandered over.

'Hi. You look scared.'

I instantly recognized his accent. He was from Liverpool.

'It's been a long, hard day,' I replied.

'What's your name?'

'Noel.'

'They call me Swannie. What you in for, Noel?'

'They've charged me with murder.'

'Same here.'

'I didn't do it. In fact, I don't know anything about it.'

'I hear you're an ex-cop.'

With that I broke into a cold sweat, fearing the worst.

I took a deep breath. 'Yeah, I am. But I resigned before all this happened.'

'I've heard you've had it rough since you've been in here.'

'Yeah.'

'Don't worry, Noel. I'll show you the ropes. We're all in the same boat.'

At last there was someone to talk to. He chatted for a while and then it was time for lights out. I got into bed feeling better as a result of Swannie's kindness. I couldn't sleep, though, because someone might attack me. I tried to convince myself that the security screw at the end of the ward wouldn't let it happen. When morning dawned I'd been awake all night and felt exhausted.

I washed and shaved. At least there were sinks, toilets and a bath in the ward, unlike the archaic facilities in the single cells. Swannie ate his breakfast with me and continued to tell me about the privileges available to a remand prisoner. You could receive food parcels, buy things and post off as many letters as you could afford.

After breakfast everyone made their beds and cleared up the ward. Then they played cards, chess, dominoes and other games. Feeling more secure, I joined three other cons and quickly learnt dominoes. It was a relief being accepted, even though like me the others were on remand.

As usual, the talk soon switched to the fact that

I'd been a cop. They all thought I must be an expert on the law.

One of the cons, Jim, had stabbed his girlfriend. 'Do you think I'll get life, or less for diminished responsibility?' he asked.

'Depends on your lawyers and medical reports.' The truth was, I hadn't a clue. Still, it satisfied him.

The exercise bell went and, with my new-found acceptance, I decided to join the others. Outside I tasted fresh air for the first time in days, walking round in convoy. We were about six abreast and tightly packed. The screws were dotted around, watching us.

Suddenly I felt a blow to my kidney area and seething pain shot through my body. I was fighting for breath. I heard someone behind say, 'Bastard cop', then felt a second blow. I fell to the ground in excruciating pain. As I lay there the other cons either walked over me or kicked me as they passed.

I tried to muster the strength to stand up, but the sheer volume of cons walking over me kept me down. At last I could breathe again and I swallowed great gulps of air. Then I felt hands on the shoulders.

'Get up, Noel. Come on, lad, get up.' Someone was pulling me with all his strength. Another hand grabbed me and I was on my feet. My legs buckled under the shock and pain and I was swaying from side to side. My rescuers had me gripped tightly, and we moved forward.

'Keep going, lad.' I recognized the voice. Swannie. He and another con were holding me.

The bell went and we returned to the ward. I sat on my chair, shaking and in pain. 'How much more can I take?' I thought. The screws hadn't noticed the attack. If it hadn't been for Swannie and Jim, what would have happened?

I nervously pulled out a cigarette. How stupid I'd been to think I was safe because a few people had talked to me. This was a different world. I'd never imagined so much hatred and bitterness towards authority. Things were getting worse for me by the day. The cons had hit and kicked me in the right places. No blood was shed. All I was left with was horror, shock, fear—and bruising.

Swannie came and asked how I was feeling.

'Lousy.'

'You'll have to fight back.'

'How can I when they attack me from behind?'

'You'll have to learn, Noel. If you sense trouble, hit out first.'

'OK, I'll remember that.'

We continued chatting. Swannie was expert on surviving the laws of the jungle. He'd grown up in Liverpool backstreets and had served his apprenticeship in personal survival. He was my age—22—but more mature and with greater experience of the system.

After a few days I went on exercise again. I stuck close to Swannie and the time passed without violence. Cons made nasty remarks but I ignored them. It was obvious that the others respected Swannie and that he wasn't to be tangled with.

Monday came with the usual procedure of going

into the sweat-box and then off to Lancaster. At least I'd be out of Risley for a few hours. McHugh had no new information. He told me I'd have to wait for the committal proceedings, when the police would present my case to the court, who in turn would decide whether to send me for trial.

'When'll that be?'

'When the police have finished their enquiry.'

My heart sank. 'Well, you'd better make noises. I'm the victim of constant attacks in Risley. It's destroying me.'

He assured me he was doing all he could.

'What's the point?' I thought. 'Nobody believes anything I say.'

The days seemed to get longer as prison routine ground on—the same daily existence determined for you minute by minute. I wrote to my parents and friends, trying to make things look better than they were, but I soon ran short of topics. They even controlled your writing. If you told the truth the censor sent it back for rewriting. Even the ward screws wrote a daily report on our behaviour.

Later that week I was taken to see the senior medical officer—a psychiatrist. He said that everyone remanded on a murder charge had to have a medical report to present to the court. He took down my history, then asked subtle questions about the charge. I told him I was totally innocent and therefore couldn't give him any information. He accepted my reply but continued the questioning.

It was like a game of mental chess lasting two hours and leaving me exhausted. It was ironic to hear that the report would be impartial. How *could* it be impartial when the interview had been inside prison and I wouldn't be given access to it?

The interview ended.

'Would you like something to help you sleep?' the doctor offered.

I shook my head. 'No, thanks,' I said. 'My conscience is clear. Sleep's only interrupted by the nightmare of this place.'

I'd seen lots of cons on the ward getting their tots of tranquillisers. They weren't going to turn *me* into a junkie. Besides, many of the cons were bleary-eyed during the day, incapable of rational speech. I wanted to know everything happening to me, not escape from it under drugs.

The following afternoon Swannie was lying on his bed. The ward screw commanded him to sit on a chair. Swannie told him to get stuffed. An argument began. The screw pressed the alarm bell and within seconds ten more screws arrived. They carried Swannie out to cries of abuse as Swannie tried to free himself.

One screw shouted, 'Get the padded cell ready for this bastard. We'll show him who's boss.'

Everything in me felt the injustice of the place. All Swannie had done was lie on the bed in the afternoon. Risley represented oppression and showed a total lack of care or understanding of the unbearable position of remand prisoners.

The weekend arrived. My parents came—it was their first visit since I'd been at Risley. They looked well and I sat opposite them to talk. To my disgust, the discipline screw who'd escorted me sat in the corner of the room. We weren't to enjoy any privacy. We couldn't discuss the case because the screw would put it down and pass it on to the police, who in turn would undermine our intent. This may have been speculation on my part, but the system breeds paranoia.

My dad said that McHugh had engaged a top defence lawyer. McHugh was also trying to get an early date for the committal proceedings. I found the visit frustrating because of the guardian.

I turned to the screw. 'We'd like some time on our own.'

'Sorry, I don't make the rules. Not allowed.'

My mother said it didn't matter. There was no way I could tell them of the treatment I'd suffered. It'd only add to their worries. I put on a brave face.

My parents seemed as much in the dark as me. As far as they knew, no primary evidence had come to light—indeed, it couldn't. They'd got the wrong man and by now must have realized it.

Just before they left, my dad casually mentioned that my younger brother, Paul, had been interviewed several times by the police. Paul had seemed disturbed afterwards but couldn't talk about it. The only thing he'd said was that I'd borrowed a jacket from him and returned it around the time of the murder enquiry. He'd made a statement to the police about the jacket and the police had taken it for forensic tests.

I returned to the ward, a little dejected at seeing

my parents leave. It had been refreshing talking to them. I was baffled why the police had to interview my brother and take his jacket away with them. Obviously my clothes had revealed nothing, so they were looking for anything to tie me in with the crime. I felt excited about suing them for wrongful arrest. At last the truth was surfacing and I'd be cleared.

Since Swannie's departure from the ward I'd kept myself isolated, only speaking to the other cons when spoken to. I passed messages and cigarettes to Swannie via the hospital orderly (another con). Swannie was out of the strip cell and in a single cell on the ground floor. Later I saw him at exercise, so that was my cue to exercise again in safety.

Weeks drifted by. Every seven days I was escorted to Lancaster and remanded again. On May 6, 1970 I learned that committal proceedings would take place the following week.

After being remanded for another week, I met McHugh for an extended interview. He showed me statements and depositions from the prosecution and questioned me about them. This was painful. Although the statements were limited in number, they'd obviously been carefully selected. The civilian statements were factual and speculative, except Thornton's and Bamborough's from the Beach Club, and to some extent Mr Lingwood's from the taxi company, which were damning to me.

I couldn't believe what I read. Why wasn't the truth coming out? McHugh asked questions about the statements and I answered as well as I could. It was difficult to remember things that had taken place nine or ten weeks previously. When it came to police statements about my interview at Lancaster, I had instant recall. McHugh drew up a statement of my answers and I asked what he thought of the prosecution case.

'It seems they've got nothing more than circumstantial evidence.'

'They couldn't have anything else. I never did it,' I said. 'What happens now?'

'The prosecution present their case next week and will decide whether to commit you for trial.'

'But most of these statement aren't true,' I protested. 'Surely the magistrates will see through them?'

On the return trip I wrestled to recall the details of the statements. The way the police had knitted their statements together was unbelievable. *Why me? Why me?* That's all I could think.

I spent the following days in depression as I tried to untangle the web of lies that had been spun around me. My frustration was immense—I was confined to Risley, cut off from the outside world, and all I could do was rely on my lawyer's professional opinion that all was going well for me.

At last 13 May came and I was escorted for committal proceedings at South Lonsdale Magistrates' Court in Lancaster Castle. I was excited that this could be my last day in custody.

We arrived at two o'clock and I met with McHugh.

He was optimistic. The police hadn't released any further statements to him. The proceedings started, with the prosecution handing in statements from twenty-eight witnesses, and a further five who were to give evidence at the proceedings.

The prosecution called Paul Fellowes. My heart sunk. Why call my younger brother? Paul told the court I'd borrowed his jacket and returned it around the date of the murder. He went on to say I'd spoken to him on the phone, saying someone was pestering me and I was going to 'have him'. His evidence ended as he told the court he'd seen me wear a purple cravat on occasions.

As Paul replied to the prosecutor's questions, he was white with fear and stuttered. My heart went out to him. I felt strongly that the police had set him up with the statement he'd signed—the last two elements were complete fabrication. Not only were they trying to stitch *me* up, now they'd implicated my brother.

Other civilian witnesses testified: Dr Beeson, the pathologist; Mrs Hockenhull, the deceased's cleaner; Mrs Barrett, a friend of the dead man; and Mrs Lingwood, wife of the manager of the taxi business I worked for. She gave evidence about the missing taxi records for my work on Tuesday 24 February.

McHugh challenged all the witnesses but there was little he could do as none of the police gave evidence. The magistrates didn't hesitate to commit me to trial at Lancaster Assizes to answer the charge of murder.

I saw McHugh afterwards. I was furious at what the police had done to my brother. 'He's only nine-teen, and the police have conveniently tied him into the case.'

McHugh told me to calm down. The trial would expose the police to cross-examination and the defence lawyers would get to the truth, he said.

I returned to Risley despondent. What I'd witnessed in court was a farce. I was back in the nightmare. There was no freedom, no let-up in threats from the cons and no hope of release before the trial. I was fenced in, totally insecure.

Risley had damaged me deeply. Once carefree, I was now introverted, fearful and depressive. The system had turned me inside-out. All I could do was hold myself together until the trial.

6 Expert Witnesses

The morning of 22 June, 1970 arrived to the usual sound of screws bellowing, 'Slop out.' I felt excited. It was the day of my trial. 'This is surely the end of the nightmare when the truth finally gets told and my freedom won,' I told myself.

After a rushed breakfast, I was whisked to reception where I changed into my normal clothes. I wouldn't have won the year's best-dressed man award, but I knew wasn't being tried for the clothes I wore.

My greatest disappointment was my hair. The previous night the ward screw cut it—and I could see in the mirror I'd been well and truly shorn.

Locked in the sweat-box I considered the day ahead with renewed optimism. Before long the discipline screws came, I was cuffed and led to the police vehicle.

My optimism took a sudden jolt as the vehicle rounded the last corner and began the uphill climb towards Lancaster Castle. Being a local, I knew some of the fearful legends surrounding this 700-year-old castle. It had the dubious distinction of sending more people to the gallows than any other castle in the land.

Perhaps the most famous trial at Lancaster was that of the Pendle witches—ten women from the hills of East Lancashire who practised strange, pagan rites. They paid with their lives, and one is thought to be buried outside the gateway. The trials of Timothy Burke, the last man to be publicly hanged in Britain, and Richard Peddar, the last to die on the gruesome 'short-drop rope', took place here in the 1850s.

There'd been two areas of execution—a hanging corner visible to passers-by and a yard on which the sun never shone. It was said that gas workmen uncovered a skeleton near the hanging corner. All this only increased my sense of unease.

I was shepherded into an anteroom, then guided into a sweat-box more confined than those at Risley. For an hour I sat with only a glimmer of light piercing my gloom. I could hear the screws settling down for a cup of tea—but I was excluded from the tea party.

Suddenly the door opened. 'It's time to go, Fellowes. You're going to meet your Queen's Counsel.'

I ascended a flight of stairs and met Mr Ernest Sanderson Temple QC—the man my destiny depended on. He was renowned in the north, having had a wealth of experience. Educated at Oxford, he reached the rank of Lieutenant-Colonel in the Border Regiment in India and Burma. During his service he became a barrister-at-law and took on his first case in 1945.

After the initial pleasantries, the bombshell was dropped: 'Have you considered pleading guilty to manslaughter?'

My jaw dropped in amazement.

'Possibly you'd get as little as five years.'

I told him I couldn't possibly plead guilty when I was totally innocent. He pledged full support, but my confidence was shaken by his suggestion. As he disappeared to take his place in court I felt like a pawn in a game of legal chess. The stakes were high—yet I didn't know the rules.

I was summoned to the dock. Nervousness gripped me once more. Four steps led to the centre stage of the oak-panelled courtroom—a dock fringed by spiked rails. Every seat seemed occupied. An excited chatter filled the air until I appeared, then a hush crept over the courtroom.

All eyes were on me, some in pity, others in persecution. Flanked by screws I sat waiting instruction. The court rose as His Honour Mr Justice Bernard Caulfield took his place.

The court clerk's voice echoed around the chamber: 'Keith Noel Fellowes, you are charged that you at Overton in the County of Lancaster, between the 23th and 26th days of February 1970 did murder Harold John Driscoll Parkinson, against the peace of our Sovereign Lady Queen, her Crown and dignity. How do you plead? Do you plead guilty or not guilty?'

Trembling, I responded, 'Not guilty, my lord.'

The prosecuting counsel, Mr Godfrey Heilpern QC, opened the case against me. I felt detached. I remembered a previous committal hearing when the prosecutor was forced to admit that there was purely circumstantial evidence against me. Heilpern's opening address made no such comment.

He produced a motive. I'd been under a 'very strong impression' that I was being followed by a private investigator. My marriage had broken up and I'd been 'carrying on' with another woman. My romantic activities were being charted by Harold Parkinson, probably employed by my mother-in-law.

Heilpern went into the grim details of how the body was found. As he spelt out the full horror of the way Parkinson had died, many eyes returned to me to detect any giveaway expressions on my face. There were none. I had no shame over a killing I wasn't involved in.

The jury—seven men and five women—were told how the body was found by Parkinson's friend, Mr Darby. His graphic description must have touched the jury's emotions. He'd last seen Parkinson alive at 9.30a.m. on Tuesday 24 February when he called at his house.

Mrs Hockenhull, the cleaner, had an even later sighting of him. She'd been cleaning when her daughter, Patricia, called at 3.30p.m. He gave them drinks, then at 4p.m.—'I remember the time because he set his clock right'—the two women left.

Evidence of three sightings the following day was brought to the court's attention, though the jury were urged into disregarding these statements in preference to others.

One came from pathologist Dr Brian Beeson. His postmortem analysis concluded that death occurred between 7a.m. and midnight on 25 February. He then dismantled his precise argument by saying it was 'possible that death could have occurred as early as the evening of the 24th'.

The prosecution was leaning towards Tuesday 24 February as the day of the death because I had a cast-iron alibi for the 25th and 26th. Heilpern stressed that 'the deceased was dead by Wednesday morning'. How was he so certain when Dr Beeson—an expert—couldn't be? The answer was that I'd been alone for most of the time from 6.30 on Wednesday evening until 2.50 in the morning.

Police had questioned my boss, Gerry Lingwood. 'I arranged with Fellowes that he'd look after the office that night (24th) up to midnight; he was there at 6.30p.m. I returned to the office at 12.05 to do the night-time office work. Fellowes was there then. I believe he was stood up answering the phone. He was wearing my fawn Gannex raincoat and I told him to take it off. He told me to hang on while he took his money out of a pocket. He then hung it over the office partition.'

Lingwood told how I'd left to pick up fares in Morecambe, returned at 2.50a.m. and remained there until about 5.30a.m. The prosecution would later say I'd had ample time during those hours to commit the murder.

Lingwood had outlined to police the system of

drivers filling in log-sheets for fares taken and office staff transferring these to a daily record-sheet. It was suggested to the jury that some of these office-sheets had been removed and that I'd destroyed them so my movements couldn't be monitored.

Lingwood said: 'One day just after Fellowes had left his wife, a man came to my home—I presumed he was a private detective—and asked where Fellowes lived. I later told Fellowes about this and I seem to remember in the conversation that he said there was a private detective at Overton and one at Lancaster. Fellowes also said that he thought for a long time that someone had been following him.'

He also recalled: 'I've been shown a purple-coloured silk scarf and it's very similar in colour and material to one that I've seen worn by Fellowes. The last time I'd seen him wearing this scarf was about three weeks ago, before the Overton incident.'

Dr Alan Clift, the forensic scientist, gave evidence on bloodstains found at the house—all group A, resembling the victim's, not mine. He then told of his intricate analysis of other samples taken at the scene, none of which linked me with the victim.

But there was one opaline green wool fibre found under Parkinson's fingernail that left doubt in the jury's minds. It was similar to fibres in the lining of the Gannex raincoat I'd worn occasionally at the taxi office. Under cross-examination, Dr Clift was forced to admit that a green sweater found near the body contained the same fibres.

Dr Clift also referred to a wool fibre from Parkinson's shoe that was similar to one found on a pair of black trousers I wore. Again, under cross-examination, Dr Clift admitted the pink fibre was very common and that the jury themselves might well find a similar one on their persons at any time.

My QC suggested to Dr Clift that he might have expected more forensic evidence, considering the degree of violence used. 'The deceased was by no means a small man and was a thickset sort of person. It's inconceivable that he'd have placidly allowed himself to have been tied up in the manner indicated and indeed evidence shows that considerable violence was used. One would have thought that whoever committed the crime would have shown some sign of injury himself.'

One of my defence lawyers wrote in his brief, 'The surprising thing in the forensic evidence is the large number of matters which it doesn't mention and which normally are available in a trial such as this.' He added that, even allowing for the fact that as a former police officer I'd know how to deal with fingerprints, the absence of such evidence counted in my favour.

That comment touched on an issue that was to worry the jury: A former policeman would know how to cover his tracks.

My expectation of being acquitted rose as I realized the lack of forensic evidence and the fact that, though the police had examined all my clothes, not a 'pinhead' of Parkinson's blood was ever traced.

Dr Clift said he'd tried to tie himself up in the same way as the deceased but couldn't tie the cable around his wrists. I felt my QC had verbally tied up Dr Clift—his contribution to the case was almost irrelevant.

My confidence took a dive when I saw my 18-year-old girlfriend, Lynn Hazelgrave, enter the witness-stand. It was an ordeal for a young girl, and the prosecution were determined not to make it easy for her. Heilpern questioned her on details of our relationship—though I couldn't see what bearing that had on the case. Some of her answers to his probing questions didn't measure up to his expectation and he applied to the judge to treat her as a 'hostile witness'. But Lynn continued to answer the only way she knew how—with the truth.

Lynn described how she first met me in August 1969. She said I was always joking about life and I'd made jocular remarks about the case before being arrested, including, 'Watch out, you might be sitting next to a murderer!' She reported a time when the two of us heard noises outside her home. The prosecution suggested it might have been a private investigator, but she said it could have been anybody.

She was adamant in her denial of seeing me wear a purple cravat, recently or at any other time.

The Crown tried to blacken her character but she talked frankly and candidly about our relationship. She left the witness-box with the same simple dignity with which she'd entered it.

Lynn's father, James Hazelgrave, was next. He'd

welcomed me into the family home. I'd been honest with him about my marriage break-up and he'd respected that. My jocular remarks were in keeping with my happy-go-lucky style of life. The last time he'd seen me I'd joked, 'Don't forget, future address Walton jail.' He hadn't taken it seriously and didn't read into it what the prosecution sought to.

My defence was looking sound. But the most grievous damage came from two men—Carey Thornton and John Bamborough.

Thornton was the 23-year-old manager of the Beach Club, a gambling den. Occasionally I'd driven him and Bamborough home in the early hours. I was dumbfounded when he alleged that he and I met in the club's Shell Bar a couple of days before the death.

'I asked him about his marriage difficulties and he told me he'd been followed by a man named Parkinson who was a private detective. He'd mentioned this man on an occasion about four weeks previously as someone who was following him around. He thought his mother-in-law had employed Parkinson. He said to me, "The other night I saw Parkinson on the promenade by the central pier at Morecambe. I tackled him about following me and then I did him up." '

Thornton hadn't finished. He talked of another meeting in the same club, along with Lynn and Bamborough, on March 7. Thornton alleged I said, 'There seem to be a lot of things pointing at me,' and, 'I made three trips to Overton in the taxi that night.'

The jury were now being urged to believe that I'd clashed with Parkinson because he was tailing me and that I'd been in his village on the night of the killing.

There was one more nasty surprise from the club manager. 'He always wore an open-necked shirt and in place of a tie a purple-coloured silk scarf of an identical colour to the one shown to me.'

Bamborough was a 30-year-old bouncer at the Beach Club. He loyally confirmed his boss's statement, adding, 'Fellowes didn't seem worried, more likely annoyed at being pulled in by the police.' Bamborough's integrity as a witness came in for a battering when my QC revealed that he'd once been arrested by me for an alleged motoring offence. He'd had other confrontations with the law, and the jury were left to decide about this man's credentials as an impartial witness.

I was outraged at these men's version of events. At the end of that day's business in court, the pendulum had swung away from me. Was the Crown convincing the jury I was a murderer?

7 Gagged and Bound

The next morning my brother Paul gave evidence. It was distressing to hear what he'd said at the committal proceedings repeated here. I suspected he was only standing there because of police pressure.

He was pale and too agitated to glance in my direction. My defence lawyers had underestimated the impact of a suspect's brother giving evidence against him. In their pre-trial brief they wrote, 'He may very well have had his memory refreshed by the time of the trial, but his evidence doesn't amount to very much.'

Paul told the court how he and I used to tie each other up during games as children. He described me as aggressive and related an alleged phone conversation with me. 'He said something like, "Somebody's following me but I'll have him." '

This was perhaps *the* turning-point of the trial. Although his evidence was uncorroborated, it lent credence to the earlier remarks of Thornton and

Bamborough. A tide of accusations flooded against me—and the police evidence was still to come.

The police case was interrupted before it started by my QC, who questioned the admissibility of some of their evidence. The judge cleared the jury and public gallery and, to my astonishment, I was returned to my cell.

The dispute was over the long time the police had taken to interview me at Lancaster Police Station. I'd been at the mercy of different teams of high-ranking officers right through the night.

The two QCs were apparently drawn into open combat for most of the Wednesday and Thursday morning of the trial. When the jury were asked to return to their seats, they were told, 'I rule that all evidence subsequent to 9p.m. on Sunday 8 March to breakfast time of Monday 9 March is inadmissible.' Mr Justice Caulfield added that some of my alleged remarks had been obtained by oppression.

Detective Sergeant James McEwan told how he'd first met me in the taxi office and how he'd revealed that my mother-in-law's address had been found in the victim's notebook. I'd gone with him to Memorial Hall to be photographed and fingerprinted for 'elimination purposes'. He'd shown me a photo of Parkinson and I'd said, 'I've seen him somewhere, but I can't remember where it was. It may come back to me.'

What I'd meant was that Morecambe had plenty of male pensioners—he looked like everybody's grandad.

McEwan had taken my clothes for forensic examination. He then mentioned an alleged conversation we'd had during a car trip to Memorial Hall, though I was sure we hadn't talked much.

He reported that I said, 'I did see that chap on Tuesday or Wednesday. I remember now. I think it was on the front at Morecambe in the afternoon. There's a few things I know about this chap.'

Then I was supposed to have said, 'Do me a favour and I'll do you a favour.' I'd asked if he could do anything about a speeding offence committed by Carey Thornton. I'd certainly have remembered saying that, if I *had* said it.

McEwan had also carried out time and distance trials in the Morecambe and Overton areas. It was an attempt to prove that I could have driven to Overton and killed Parkinson during the evening of the 24th or the early hours of the 25th.

My defence had done their homework here, saying that experienced taxi drivers had 'in practically each case doubled the time to do the journey from that given by the witness'.

Joe Mounsey cut an impressive figure as he strolled to the witness-box. Not waiting for the usher to pass him the card with the oath printed on it, he repeated it in deep, authoritative tones.

In spite of his outward calm, Mounsey must have had some misgivings. Most of his all-night interview with me had been ruled inadmissible by the judge. He related his earlier interview with me at the Memorial Hall:

'Who was the private detective at Overton?'

'That was him, Parkinson. He couldn't mind his own business. He's a sadist.'

'What makes you say he's a sadist?'

'That came second-hand.'

'Do you know Parkinson?'

'I've seen him.'

'How well do you know him?'

'Not socially.'

'But you've met him?'

(Long silence.)

'I've nothing to say.'

'I repeat, you've met him?'

'I've never met him.'

'I repeat again, you've met him?'

(Long silence.)

'He was following me. It was her fault.'

'Whose?'

'Her mother's.'

'When did you last have a conversation with Parkinson?'

(No reply.)

'I believe you've met him recently.'

'I haven't had a conversation with him that I can recollect.'

'When did you last meet him—was it last week? I think you met him the night he died. I think you went to his house.'

'I don't know—I don't know him socially.'

'I think you met him last week, the night he died. Did you go to his house that night?'

(No direct answer.) Short discussion on domestic difficulties.

'He was following me that night. I'll speak to my wife before I do or say anything about this. She's the only one I trust. It's all her mother's fault anyway. She thinks it's her kids, not our kids. I was lucky to have handed in my resignation to the police force first before the trouble started.'

'Tell us what's on your mind. What was your intention with Parkinson? Why was he following you?'

'You don't understand. He was everywhere.'

'Tell us what your intentions were with Parkinson. I think you went to his house last week.'

(No direct answer.)

'Did you kill him?'

'He was following me. My wife'll tell me what to say.'

Later, on the journey to Lancaster:

'You wouldn't have caught me without the help of the public. You've got nothing from my fingerprints and my clothing, have you?'

'Why don't you tell us what you did to Parkinson?'

'If I told you, that'd be an admission and I'd sooner talk to my wife first.'

At Lancaster police station:

'Now tell me what you did to Parkinson the night he died.'

'He seemed to be everywhere. I saw him when I was in Euston Road. I said, "Are you following me?" He mumbled something and I swore at him.'

'That wasn't the night he died, though?'

'No.'

'Did you hit him on that occasion?'

'No.'

'But what about the night Parkinson died?'

'That'd be an admission. I met him that night. It was in the centre of Morecambe. My wife'll tell me what to say.'

'What night was it that he died?'

'It's in some corner at the back of my mind. What do I do? I can't tell you until I've seen my wife. I trust her. What do I do?'

'Do you want your wife to tell you whether to tell the truth or not?'

'Yes.'

'I thought you said you didn't know him. Then you said he was following you. What's the story? I believe you went to his house that night. You said you met him the night he died, in the centre of Morecambe. What happened after that? What did you do to him?'

(Glancing at another detective): 'If he's going to write it all down I'm saying no more.'

The rest of the interview—which took up ten pages—was inadmissible.

Mounsey was adamant that the interview had been conducted in a proper manner.

'There was no rapid-fire questioning and I didn't exercise any pressure to induce him to make any admissions,' he said. He added that I hadn't asked for a solicitor at any time while in the interview room.

My QC challenged him on his 'brusque' interview technique and took issue over his showing me harrowing photos of the dead man. My defence claimed Mounsey had tried to 'frighten' me into confessing.

Mounsey deflected the barrage of criticism in the manner of a professional detective. He claimed his persistent questioning had been justified by the seriousness of the charge and the strong suspicions against me.

My hostility towards this man hadn't subsided by the time he left the box to monitor what was to be my defence.

After lunch on day four of the trial, Thursday, Sanderson Temple told me he had no intention of calling any defence witnesses, myself included. I was aghast.

He explained that I'd appear as a solitary figure denouncing every witness as a liar. Who would the jury believe—me, in a fragile psychological and emotional state, or police officers with unimpeachable credentials?

At first I refused his advice. He countered that the Crown under cross-examination would 'rip me to shreds', undoing all his previous good work. Support for his view came from both junior counsel and my own lawyer, McHugh.

With a heavy heart I asked for time to consider. But there were only minutes left before we were all due back in court. So I agreed to their plan, even though everything inside told me to do exactly the opposite. It was a decision I regretted for many years.

The prosecution case completed, my QC announced that there would be no defence submissions other than his own summing-up. There was an audible gasp from the public gallery and a puzzled expression on Heilpern's face.

On Friday morning, before counsel gave their final addresses, I was asked to sign a statement: 'I have been advised that I am entitled to give evidence on my own behalf at my trial and I have decided that I do not wish to give evidence.'

Heilpern, as prosecutor, said he'd established a motive—I'd killed Parkinson in a fit of rage because he'd been following me as a private investigator hired by my mother-in-law. He claimed that my movements had been shielded by the 'convenient' removal of record-sheets. He stressed that several witnesses seemed convinced that the purple material gagging Parkinson had been my cravat. There were also the alleged verbal admissions, jocular remarks and forensic evidence on fibres to consider.

Sanderson Temple's response was that the evidence against me was circumstantial and didn't stand up to close inspection. Out of the hundreds interviewed, no witnesses had seen me with Parkinson or even near his home. The joking remarks were to be taken merely as jokes. There'd been no reason to call defence witnesses because the prosecution had failed to substantiate 'beyond any reasonable doubt' that I was involved in the crime.

His final remark to the jury was, 'Direct evidence against my client disappears like snow in the sun.'

A weekend of hell lay in store for me back at Risley. On Monday my fate would be sealed one way or the other. As I mulled over the week-long court case I concluded that nearly everyone had it in for me.

Visitors tried to comfort me that I'd soon be a free man. This was the view shared by my counsel as the judge began his five-hour summing-up:

'I'm sorry I've had to go into such detail, but in a case where there's been a mysterious death it may be that it's the little bits of evidence—and perhaps the little utterances made by the accused—which you will find the most important.'

He asked the jury to consider all the evidence carefully and to assess all witnesses and police. Had the Crown proved that I'd been hostile to Parkinson in any way—either alone or with someone else? If I intended to do grievous bodily harm or kill him then I was guilty of murder.

'Don't be satisfied with suspicion. Don't worry if in your minds you have strong suspicions but you find you can't bring yourself to say you're sure. Just treat your deliberations judiciously, without fear, ill will or sympathy.'

Before the jury retired, they were told that I had no previous convictions for any criminal act.

In the sweat-box, time rolled agonisingly by. After an hour, the escort screw opened the door flap and said, 'Someone in there [the jury] must be rooting for you.' He added that my mother had handed him a book to pass on to me. It was a blue hardback Bible.

Although not a Christian I was desperate enough to try anything. Clasping the Bible in both hands I knelt down. 'God, if you're really there, you know I'm innocent of this man's death. If you convince the jury of the truth, I'll believe in you for ever.'

It was a crude deal but it offered me some solace. I put the Bible down, covered my face with my hands and repeatedly pleaded, 'Not guilty, not guilty'. It was a vain hope that somehow the message would get through to the twelve most important people in the world at that time.

The news that the jury had reached a verdict brought me back to reality. I laboured with every breath as the jury took their seats. The foreman—a tall, dark-haired man with an expressionless face—stood as the clerk asked whether they'd reached a decision. 'Yes,' he replied.

I thought my chest would cave in under the pressure of that moment.

'Do you find the defendant, Keith Noel Fellowes, guilty or not guilty of the murder of Harold Parkinson?'

'Not guilty.'

My lifeblood returned. I turned to make my way out of the dock. I saw my parents, their faces alight with happiness approaching delirium. But my progress was halted by the screws on either side of me, who kept a grip on my arms.

Somewhere in the court, the drama was continuing. Suddenly, I noticed the foreman standing and recording a verdict of 'guilty to manslaughter'.

My elation was wiped away amid an outcry from the public gallery. The judge demanded order. My legs suddenly caved under me and my body slumped back. The screws struggled to raise me back on my feet. A silent scream lay trapped in my throat—I was going to be jailed for a crime I hadn't done.

Detective Chief Inspector William Howson made his way to the witness-box to give further details of my background. It was ironic it should be Bill Howson. He'd been head of the divisional CID when I'd been in the police. He once complimented me for a number of good arrests I'd made and he had plans to recruit me as a detective.

He described how since leaving school at 15 I'd taken various jobs before joining the Lancashire police in 1968. I'd resigned the following year because of an unsettled family life.

My QC argued for leniency. Then Mr Justice Caulfield ordered me to my feet. His voice was a punishment in itself. I half expected him to don black cap and despatch me to the gallows. He said the case had been tragic for me. The jury had found that I was 'at the very least implicated' in the tying up of Parkinson. They'd also found that I'd intended him harm and, as a result, a life had been lost.

'It would appear to be your temper which prompted you to enter this field of activity,' he said.

My legs buckled as he handed out a sentence of seven years. I doubt if it would have had more impact if he'd said seventy years. As I was hustled from the court, I saw in the gallery my mother-in-law and wife smiling. I burst into tears. Once in the sweat-box, my sobbing became uncontrollable, and every muscle started to shake involuntarily.

Despair consumed me. My parents were allowed to see me 15 minutes later but my mother was unable to speak. Her pain made mine even worse.

'They gave me seven years and I'm innocent,' said an unfamiliar voice. It was my own.

My dad guided my mother away.

Only a few months earlier I'd been carefree and happy-go-lucky. Now, I was engulfed by an uncaring, biased system, a system that dared to call itself justice.

8 Seven Years

29 June, 1970 was the blackest day of my life. All my hopes were shattered. My head was thumping like a bass drum. All my expectations of freedom had vanished in one word—*guilty*.

How could I be found guilty of a crime I didn't commit? Things like that were reserved for fiction writers.

I sat in shock, unable to control the shaking. Tears flowed. I tried to force them back but within seconds I was sobbing my heart out. They were tears of distress, insecurity and fear. Soon I regained control, spurred on by embarrassment as the screws outside looked on at the pitiful sight of a broken 22-year-old man.

'You will go to prison for seven years.' I could hear the judge's voice echoing the words. The impact was to stay with me for a long time.

One of the escort screws asked it I'd like a cup of sweet tea before the journey back to Risley. I just looked at him. My voice was suffering under the intense state of shock. The next thing I realized the screw had returned with a cup of tea.

'Now, come on, Noel. Drink this up. It'll help you get over the shock.'

He spoke in a soft, reassuring voice.

I took the cup in my shaking hands and tried to drink but finished up pouring half the contents over myself accidentally.

'Don't worry, Noel,' the screw said. 'It's understandable considering the day you've had.'

It was the first time anybody in the system had offered consolation.

Shortly after eight o'clock we left for Risley. Again I was handcuffed, but now as a convicted killer. The screws were considerate, trying to assure me that seven years wasn't really seven years.

'You'll probably do two years and get parole. At the worst you'll only get four years eight months with good behaviour.'

'I'm innocent. I should be outside,' I said.

'You'll get used to it. They'll probably put you in an open nick, you being an ex-cop.'

On they went, trying to convince me that all would be well. They were sincere in their speculation, but all I could think of were the past months of fear, stress and abuse. What was going to happen now I'd been convicted?

I'd heard rumours about life inside for ex-cops. Having just witnessed injustice first hand, I understood why cons hated police so much. Was I to be the punchbag for the cons to vent their hatred on? All I could do was hope for the best.

Back at Risley the screws announced my sentence to the senior screw.

'Not bad, Fellowes. You could have got life.'

I just gazed at him.

'Right, Fellowes, as a convicted criminal you wear grey.'

I was now a con. They fitted me out with grey clothes and escorted me back to the hospital wing. I declined a sleeping draught and walked through the ward to whispered voices.

'What'd you get?'

'Seven years.'

The more I said seven years the more daunting it sounded. I was awake all night going over the final day of the trial, trying to understand why the jury had convicted me of something I hadn't done. Everyone seemed convinced I was guilty. My constant pleas of innocence had fallen on deaf ears. I was on my own now. I decided never to trust anyone again.

The next day the remanded cons offered their consolation at my sentence and wished me luck. They knew I needed it. I was an ex-cop and many knew the consequences of such a label inside.

I was still in shock when the senior medical officer came to see me.

'Seven years isn't that bad. Don't worry, it'll all work out for you.'

He said it with a smile! The man had no idea what seven years really meant. He thought I'd done well getting only seven years. To me it was a lifetime.

'What's going to happen to me?' I asked.

'In a few days you'll be going to Walton Prison in Liverpool.'

'What then?'

'After you've been assessed, the Home Office will decide where you'll serve the rest of your sentence.'

I asked Swannie on exercise what to expect of a prison for convicted criminals. He said Risley was paradise compared to real prisons, where life was nothing less than a cattle market. He explained the need to show no fear or weakness to either screws or cons. If I did, they'd make my life even more intolerable.

Swannie was still on remand and I wished him well for the coming trial.

He shrugged his shoulders. 'What will be will be.'

What a character! He seemed to take everything as it came. But if what Swannie said about Walton was true, how was I going to cope?

On 5 July, 1970 I was told I'd be transferred to Walton Prison the following day. I felt sick and spent another sleepless night worrying about what lay in store.

The next morning I was handcuffed and put on the prison bus. We were instructed where to sit on the wooden benches. I surveyed the faces of the other cons—all looked gloomy. Everyone seemed lost in their own thoughts.

On arrival we were ushered into sweat-boxes. The graffiti on the walls represented hatred and violence. There were comments about cops, pigs and screws that made my heart sink. Swannie was right. Cops weren't the best-loved people in prisons. Immense fear gripped me as I waited to be processed.

I sat waiting my turn, desperate for a cigarette. Since being convicted a week previously, all remand privileges had been withdrawn, including the ability to buy cigarettes out of my private money. I was now paid only enough weekly to buy myself half an ounce of tobacco, two packets of papers and a box of matches. I'd already smoked the lot.

'811168 Fellowes,' a voice shouted.

'That's me.'

The door opened and a screw said, 'Follow me.'

I was processed, given clothes and bedding and taken to the main prison. The door opened into the main prison block and I was hit by the volume of noise—cons shouting, their voices echoing through the long cell-blocks. Hundreds of cons were walking about on various landings with chamber pots and jugs.

'You're lucky, Fellowes,' the screw said. 'It's slop-out time, then association.'

'Oh, really.' I hadn't a clue what he meant.

Walton was a Victorian prison, built in a star shape, with four wings going off from the centre. Each wing had four landings with cells either side.

There was a mesh screen covering the open space on the second level, protecting anyone on the ground floor (the 'ones') where association and recreation facilities were located. It also saved anyone who decided to jump off the fours, and it protected the discipline screws from any objects thrown by cons off the threes and fours.

I was allocated a single cell in B wing. 'You're lucky again, Fellowes. Everyone's three in a cell here, but seeing you're a long-termer I've given you a single cell.'

A screw took me to my cell.

'There you are, lad. You'd better get yourself organized.'

My first impression was one of horror. The cell was six feet by 12 feet with brick walls painted in appalling colours. The floor was tiled and the place smelt of damp. The furniture consisted merely of a bed with a foam mattress, a wooden chair, a chamber pot, a water jug and a plastic bowl.

What a contrast to the hospital wing as Risley! 'How could anybody be expected to survive in such conditions?' I asked myself. It was the worst form of human degradation.

My first night at Walton was sleepless. I could feel the bed springs under the foam mattress, and the pillow felt like a lump of crushed concrete.

The next day, following slopping-out and breakfast, I was escorted to the administration block for various interviews. First I met the social welfare officer. Welfare? What a joke!

Next stop was IQ and other psychological tests. I asked what they were for. The shrink said, 'They're used to assess your educational maturity and what work'll best suit you in prison.'

'They must be for something more devious than

that!' I thought. I did the IQ test but spoiled the rest of the papers. The shrink asked me why I'd done that.

'Because it's bad enough being in here, without you treating me like a guinea-pig.'

Next was the prison chaplain. All he wanted to know was my religion. I said I was christened a Protestant and wasn't a Christian by any stretch of the imagination.

The last stop was an official meeting with the assistant governor.

'811168 Fellowes,' bellowed the screw.

I was told to march into his office, stand to attention and speak my number and name. I did the necessary but was severely reprimanded.

'Sir! You always address members of staff as "sir". Start again, Fellowes.'

'811168 Fellowes, sir.'

'That's better,' said a wisp of a man sitting behind a desk double his size. 'We'll soon get you used to prison life.'

He explained that my earliest release date with remission would be the end of 1974. In between, I'd be interviewed for parole. He said I was only at Walton to be allocated to a long-term prison. That was the end of the interview and off I went back to my peter (cell).

I remained banged up for a couple of days. This was the system's way of breaking in new prisoners. It suited me as I didn't want the other cons to find out who I really was. But I was still depressed. I relived the trial daily. It all seemed brutally unjust.

Why did so many people want to put me away?

A few days later I was told by a screw that I'd been allocated to work in the canvas shop. My heart sank.

I followed the screw and inside found fifty or sixty cons eyeing me over. My insecurity rose and I started to tremble. The workshop screw told me to join a group of cons cutting up canvas. I sat down and one con showed me what to do. Then I recognized a con I'd been on remand with at Risley. He started talking to the others in his group.

Within minutes eye were staring at me. It reminded me of the Memorial Hall when I was led out by Mounsey. Danger signals were ringing in my head. He was telling them I was an ex-cop, and word was spreading.

Eventually it reached our group. A con from Liverpool said, 'Is that right, lad? You're an ex-pig?'

'Yeah, I was.'

'Well, lad, we don't like pigs.'

'Neither do I.'

With that the conversation ended. The bell went for lunchtime. I waited until last as I didn't want to be involved in any 'accidents'. They trooped out, each casting an angry glance in my direction. Then I recognized another con from Risley. He'd stabbed his girlfriend in a romantic bust-up. He walked to the exit and beckoned me over.

'Look, Noel, you're in great danger.'

'I know.'

'Listen, mate. They're planning to shiv you this afternoon. Don't come to work.'

'Shiv me?'

'Stab you, cut you up a bit.'

I feared the worst. 'Those animals want to kill me,' I thought. 'If they're out to get me, get me they will.'

I followed the procession back to the cell-block, picked up my dinner and made for the safety of my peter. I couldn't eat. The screw came to bang us up for the dinner break and I told him what had happened in the workshop.

'Leave it with me, lad.'

Half an hour later the door opened and a screw instructed me to follow him.

'You're off to see the assistant governor.'

After the usual formalities, the assistant governor said sympathetically, 'I hear you're frightened for your safety, Fellowes.'

'Yes, sir.'

'We could put you under protection on Rule 43. You'd be locked up with sex offenders on protection. You don't want that, do you?'

'No, sir. The cons'll think I'm a nonce [sex offender] as well.'

'That's right. So leave the problem in our hands.'

I started to apologize.

'No need, Fellowes. I'm aware of your problem and I'll try to sort it out this afternoon.'

Back in the peter the bell sounded for afternoon work and I could hear the doors being unlocked. My heart beat faster as the door next to mine was unlocked. Would they send me to work? Relief flooded through me as the screw left my door locked. I'd be safe for a while longer.

Mid-afternoon the door opened and the assistant governor entered.

'Well, Fellowes. We've found a temporary solution. You'll be transferred to the hospital wing until you're allocated to a long-term prison. OK?'

'Yes, sir.'

He left and another screw said, 'Pack your things. You're going now.'

In the hospital wing I was allocated a single peter and banged up. The facilities were far superior, and I was safe again. But how long could I avoid a real encounter with the cons who wanted to get me?

In the evening I felt really low, wondering how I could survive the daily torment, fear and mental anguish. Everything I'd treasured in life was gone for ever. Mine was a hopeless existence.

I wallowed in self-pity. Was this my destiny— insecurity and fear? I couldn't stand it for another four years. I lay on my bed, knees up to my chest, crying my heart out, biting the end of the pillow in sheer desperation. I decided there was no future in being locked away physically and mentally. I'd top myself.

I noticed a conduit on the ceiling. It seemed secure so I tore a sheet up to make a noose. I tied the sheet to the conduit and put the noose around my neck. With tears, I jumped off the bed. Just my luck—the conduit came adrift from the ceiling and I ended up on the floor with nothing more than a ricked neck.

Now I'd damaged prison property and could lose

part of my remission. I took the sheet off and banged the conduit back in place with my fist. The sheet was a definite problem. I lay in bed trying to work out a way of changing it without the screws knowing.

The attempt to top myself had at least broken my emotional crisis. Now I was thinking more rationally.

The next morning after slop-out and breakfast I was visited by the senior medical officer.

'Any problems?'

'No, sir.'

With that he left. It was an hour later when the senior hospital screw walked in.

'You feeling all right, Fellowes?' he asked.

'Yes, sir.'

'What happened to the conduit?'

'What do you mean?'

'Looks as though someone's been tampering with it.'

My stomach turned over. Eagle eyes had spotted my misdemeanour.

'Why don't you tell me what happened?'

I gave up and told him about my distress the previous night and my circumstances since my arrest.

He looked at me, unmoved. 'I'm fully aware of your circumstances. That's why you're in this hospital wing. I'm here to help you. If you get like that again, ask to see me.'

'Thank you, sir.'

'We'll keep this incident to ourselves. Give me the sheet and I'll see to it.'

He left with the two strips of sheet. What a relief!

At least there was one screw who showed under-standing. Just sharing my anxiety had made me feel better. And he acted in *my* interests instead of the authority's.

Since my arrival at Walton, I'd kept my letter-writing just to my parents and my lawyer, McHugh. The censor must have been sick of reading my pleas of innocence and injustice. I filled in a form to appeal against conviction and sentence. But weeks passed with no word back.

At last McHugh wrote saying he'd sought counsel's advice. I couldn't appeal against conviction because there'd been no new evidence. Although I'd been given a fair trial, I *could* appeal against sentence. But seven years wasn't a harsh sentence considering the severity of the crime.

I drifted back into depression. The appeal had been my last hope—now even that was lost. I'd have to live with the injustice of my conviction and sentence. The faceless judiciary had closed my file.

I went though the motions of appealing against sentence but, as expected, I received a refusal. I wrote to McHugh saying I'd continue to protest my innocence and—however long it took—one day I'd clear my name. I never heard from McHugh again.

Three months into my sentence a crime took place 100 miles away in Warsop, Nottinghamshire. I knew nothing about it at the time. But, like so many other factors in my case, its importance only came to the surface later.

In a wages office in Warsop Town Hall, council clerk Neal Hunt was sitting at a desk when three men crept in. A gloved hand was put over his mouth and a voice said, 'Don't struggle and you won't get hurt.' The clerk was dragged into a corner where his ankles and wrists were tied with calico bandage and his mouth taped. The men took £660 in wages from an unlocked safe and left.

On the train back to Manchester the haul was split into three. Two of the men—Lenny Pilot and Billy Clark—got rid of the evidence by hurling the empty wage packets from the train window.

Pilot, a salesman, and Clark, a small-time crook, had plenty to celebrate. The information about the Warsop job had been spot-on. They decided to use the source again. The three had worked together efficiently and now had £220 each.

The days locked in my peter seemed to get longer. Being banged up for 23 hours a day only added to the torment of my mind. There were few welcome breaks in the monotony of killing time.

My parents' visits brought me back to reality for a couple of hours, but the cost was heartbreaking. Their visits reminded me of all I'd lost, and it took me days to get over them.

By September 1970 I'd become thoroughly introverted. I'd spend the best part of every day reliving the arrest, the remand and the trial. A cancer of hatred for the witnesses formed deep inside me. I fed the hatred with evil thoughts and the desire for revenge. I wanted them to taste what

I'd suffered—fear, violence, intimidation and mental torture. Then they'd realize the cost of their carefully selected words.

I was totally embittered against the police, courts, prison authorities and everyone who'd taken part in my incarceration. I was changing from a passive individual into an aggressive monomaniac with an ambition to survive the sentence and take revenge.

On 14 October, 1970 I was informed that I'd be leaving Walton for Wakefield top security prison the next day. Why top security? I remember on the way back from the trial the screws saying I'd probably go to an open nick, seeing I was an ex-cop.

I'd been in solitary for three months. Now they were putting me among top security cons. There was no arguing. I was merely a faceless number.

Wakefield was 200 miles from my family, but that wasn't considered. The system had dealt me a raw deal—all because I continued to plead my innocence. People think that all cons protest their innocence. The truth is that most admit their guilt and get on with their bird.

For me, Wakefield represented another challenge. I sank on the bed in nervous anticipation of what tomorrow would bring.

9 Doing Bird

October 15 had arrived, the day of my departure from Walton. I packed my belongings and gave my peter one last look over. For three months it had been the scene of much anguish. Only the walls knew my innermost thoughts and fears.

The senior screw, who'd helped me through the early weeks at Walton, opened up and announced it was time to go.

'Best of luck, Fellowes. I hope you succeed in the future.'

'Thanks.'

In reception I changed back into my own clothes. They'd been kept in a cardboard box and smelt musty. In the sweat-box the artistic graffiti reflecting Liverpool's humour hadn't changed. Some 45 minutes later I was escorted to a prison bus similar to the one I'd travelled in from Risley.

To my surprise I was with twenty other cons who were also being transferred. We were dropping some off at Manchester nick—known among criminals as the Strangeways Hotel—then on to Wakefield. They chatted about their experiences in Walton. I listened for any information about Wakefield, but none of them had done time there.

By early afternoon we'd arrived. The first thing I saw were the high walls mounted with security cameras.

In reception I received standard prison uniform— new clothes and shoes that fitted me perfectly. The screws seemed more relaxed and there wasn't the usual facility of sweat-boxes. Perhaps it was because there were only five of us.

In another room we were each photographed. They chalked my number, 811168, on a board which I held against my chest. Then a senior screw allotted our wings and peter numbers. Mine was to be a shared cell on the ones C wing.

Like Walton, Wakefield was built in a star shape with four wings. It housed 600 inmates—all doing between four years and life. The screw said we'd find the regime more relaxed than local prisons be-cause most of the cons were doing life.

Now I knew why they put me here. *They wanted to destroy me totally*. I didn't look forward to doing bird with a few hundred convicted murderers. This place had to be hell on earth.

My stomach turned over and I started to shake at the thought of the cons finding out about my police career. Was it to be a long time in solitary again?

We were then led into the main cell-block area. There was a lot of activity and noise and I felt insecure. I was introduced to the senior screw in charge of C wing. He told another screw to show me my quarters on the ones.

My dormitory was two peters hashed into one. It bedded four cons. I met the three others, who were doing six years each for various robberies.

'How long *you* doing?'

'Seven years,' I said.

'What you in for?'

'Manslaughter.'

'That's all right, as long as you're not a nonce [sex offender].'

'Don't they have a special wing for nonces here?'

'No. There's no Rule 43 here. They mix everyone together.'

I was feeling my way.

'Don't they get attacked?'

'Yeah, but you gotta be careful or the screws bust you and put you in the cooler [punishment block].'

At least I'd be safer here than in the last two nicks.

The rest of the evening we talked about Wakefield. The more I heard, the more assured I felt. The lifers were doing anything between nine and 20 years inside. So the screws stretched the rules to make life easier for themselves. The other good point was that haircuts were left to the individual; so far I'd endured a compulsory shearing every two weeks.

'Why are the ones in dorms?' I asked.

'It's a case of allocation. The lifers get the single peters first and so on down the line until your name comes up.'

Sounded fair. Anyone serving life deserved a single peter.

All the time I'd spent in solitary at Walton seemed to wash away in one evening. That night I slept well.

The next morning there was the usual routine. Even breakfast was still stodgy. The bell went for work but I stayed to be processed. It was the same procedure—welfare officer, education officer, then the deputy governor.

'Well, Fellowes. It says here you're protesting your innocence.'

'Yes, sir.'

'Good. We don't want any trouble with you, considering you're an ex-policeman. You should cope and you'll have the opportunity to study, if you want.'

'Thank you, sir.'

The interview over, I was allocated to the mailbag shop. Here I was given a thick needle, thread and canvas and told to sew nine stitches to the inch. The target for the week was to complete five bags.

After an hour I'd managed $1\frac{1}{2}$ inches. My problem was that I kept stabbing myself with the needle.

At lunchtime the screw checked my work. My stitching was wrong and I'd have to unpick it and start again. After lunch I noticed some of the other cons working feverishly and I asked why.

'If you finish more than five a week, you get a bonus.'

'How much?'

'Up to four shillings.'

I couldn't believe it. That was only enough to buy half an ounce of tobacco. I'd heard of slave labour but this was ridiculous.

By the end of the afternoon I'd managed to complete three inches, so I owed *them* money.

'Call this a day's work, Fellowes?' the screw asked.

I didn't answer.

'If you carry on like this, lad, you'll never get out of this shop.'

'Machines can do a far better job,' I replied.

'Machines aren't doing bird, and you are. We'll soon knock you into shape, Fellowes.'

Back in the dorm we all had a laugh over the incident with the screw. They agreed I'd probably be in the bag shop for years.

At six the door opened for association, when you could play darts, table-tennis or card games, or watch TV, all in the ones. New cons had to break into the cliques that had formed over several years, so I stayed in the dorm to read.

About 20 minutes later three cons entered the dorm. One stood guard at the door. I knew instantly they weren't paying me a social visit.

'We're the reception committee,' one said.

'We're going to protect you from all the animals in here,' said the other.

'Why do I need protection?'

'The news editor in B wing's been reading up your case.'

'So?'

'You're an ex-cop and cons don't like ex-cops.'

'What do you want?'

'Pay us your wages in tobacco every week and we'll make sure no harm comes to you.'

'And if I don't?'

'We'll give you a lesson in manners.'

There wasn't any chance to escape. I was terrified what they might do to me. Then I saw my metal food-tray, so I eased myself off the bed.

'You've got me in a tight corner. Whatever I do, it seems I lose.'

'You sure do,' they said laughing.

Swiftly, I leant over the bedside cabinet, wrapped my hands tightly around the tray and crashed it into the con's face. He went down, blood streaming over his face.

Before I could think, I was seeing stars. Blows raged around my head and body, and I heard something crack loudly on my face. Then I saw the floor coming up to meet me.

The blows continued and I heard through my half-conscious state, 'I'll get you for this, you bastard.'

They left and I lay there in a daze. I couldn't focus or get off the ground. I was violently sick, which aggravated my breathing. I thought I was definitely going to die.

Some time later I heard an echo in my head.

'Noel, Noel,' the voice said.

I stirred, recognizing the cold brick walls of the dorm.

'You all right, mate?' asked Joey, who shared the dorm with me.

'Yeah, sure.'

He picked me up off the floor.

'Wow, you look a mess. I'll get the others.'

Within minutes all three were present. They cleaned me up and asked what had happened. I told them the story.

'You might as well know, lads. I'm an ex-cop but I left before they stitched me up with this.'

'We already know,' said Alan. 'Makes no difference to us.'

'In future, till you've learnt the ropes, stick with us,' said Alan. 'If you injured one of them, they'll try to get you again.'

That was the last thing I wanted. I checked in the mirror and saw bruising around my eyes. When I touched my nose, pain reeled through my head. It was leaning to the left and I realized it was broken.

Joey said he'd find out who the cons were so we could plan a counterattack. I told him I wasn't interested. I had to fight my *own* battles—all I wanted were their names and peter numbers.

'It's not that easy. You're living among some real animals. They'll shiv you for a dirty look. You'll have to learn fast.'

I knew that, but I was determined to survive. I knew the laws of the jungle—the fittest and strongest survived. Now I needed to become super-fit. I decided to do gym and weightlifting twice a week. I was six foot one inch, and at this stage of my sentence I weighed 174 pounds.

The following morning my whole head was sore. I looked in the mirror and saw a horror story—two black eyes and the bridge of my nose a deep purple. Skipping breakfast, I rested a little longer.

The bell went for work and I trundled off to the mailbag shop. I doubted if I'd be able to thread a needle, let alone sew a mailbag.

As I worked, the other cons glanced at my injured head and commented to each other. The workshop screw called me over and asked what had happened.

'I fell down the stairs.'

'There must have been a lot of stairs. Come on, Fellowes, pull the other one.'

I remained silent, the other cons looking on.

'Better take you over to the sickbay, lad. Let a doctor look at you.'

'No, thanks. I'm fine. They're only bruises.'

'Bruises or not, you can't work. Come with me.'

I returned to the main prison and into the medical room. I refused the doctor but took some aspirin. The screw banged me up in my dorm and I fell asleep. At lunchtime the others offered to get me lunch but I declined.

Fifteen minutes after being banged up again, I was told the assistant governor wanted to see me.

'811168 Fellowes, sir,' I said on arrival.

'What's happened to you, Fellowes? I hear that you fell down the stairs.'

'Yes, sir.'

'That's hard to believe. There aren't any stairs on the ones.'

'I was on the twos going down to the ones and I slipped.'

'There's another inmate with a large gash on his face. Do you know anything about that?'

'No, sir.'

'This person is known to be a bully and a hard case. I think he had a go at you, Fellowes.'

'No, sir. I fell down the stairs.'

I knew if I grassed him my life would be hell.

'Very well, Fellowes. On your way. But take note —we'll be watching you.'

'Thank you, sir.'

'By the way, I've instructed the senior officer to allocate you the next single that comes up.'

'Special treatment,' I thought. 'He really means to keep an eye on me.'

I left his office proud that I'd kept quiet. I'd at least gain some respect. This had been the first day of my fightback campaign and already I was feeling better for it.

During the rest of that week I found out more about Wakefield. A weekday looked like this:

6.40a.m.	Unlock/slop out
7.00	Breakfast
8.40	Work/education block
11.15	Lunch
11.50	Lock-up (in cells)
1.10p.m.	Unlock
1.30	Work/education block
4.00	Supper

4.50	Lock up
6.00	Unlock/association/evening classes
8.30	Lock up

I was ultra-cautious, making sure I was always near a wall and could see what was in front and behind me. Joey told me the names of my attackers and their locations. On association one night he pointed them out to me. I took a mental picture and planned my revenge.

Saturday arrived to the sound of cons busy cleaning out their peters. It was the usual Saturday procedure. The cons on the fours, threes and twos would shake their blankets over the landings and we on the ones would try to contend with the dust. Most cons kept their peters immaculate.

The rest of the morning involved association. At 10 the dart school would start up—anything from fifteen to twenty cons playing round-the-clock darts. The first to finish won a cigarette from all the other players. To listen to them you'd have thought they were playing for the World Cup.

Then there was the table-tennis school. The winner always stayed on the table. Some of the cons had perfected their game over the years. Newcomers would be given a 15-point start and still lose! Table-tennis was noisy, echoing through the wing and disturbing the old lags (cons who'd done several stretches inside) who were having a lie-in at the weekend.

After lunch was the highlight of the week—the

soccer match. Wakefield had a good team, though they only played home matches. Visiting teams were guaranteed 600 spectators compared with the handful they were used to. The spectators always used colourful language to voice their opinion.

The tobacco barons were active at soccer matches. Prison rules allowed cons only to have two ounces of tobacco. On a good day the barons could win 30 to 40 ounces. Their runners collected the winnings and dispensed it to minders.

It was a highly organized business. If a con refused to pay his tobacco debt, the heavy mob would make him pay up. The barons would also loan tobacco with interest. Many cons mounted up large debts. The barons would demand that the con, on his next visit, send money to the baron's personal account, building up collateral to be used on release.

Sundays were a repeat of the Saturday routine, except for optional church services. Only a handful of cons attended, mainly to promote their chances of parole.

In the afternoon there was an interwing soccer match. Teams were chosen, not on merit, but on muscle power. Cons were never charged if duels happened on the soccer pitch, so many grievances were resolved without loss of remission.

Sunday evening always produced a long line outside sickbay of cons injured in the afternoon. All received the same treatment—a small tot of aspirin water. There was an unwritten rule that whatever happened on the field wasn't taken up again on the wings.

So intense was the soccer competition that B wing scrutinised cons at reception for potential players, then tried to get them allocated on to B wing.

The barons even tried to induce good players to ask for a wing transfer. It seemed like big business, but the barons were really parasites, feeding off others' weaknesses. Every few months a baron would fall and a new one emerge in a constant power struggle. Natural leaders seemed to stay in office longer than ladder-jumpers.

I always considered myself fit, but the first time I started the gym routine I thought my lungs would collapse. Every muscle ached. The instructor, Don Hemingway, certainly put us through our paces, but I warmed to him. Though he was a screw, he encouraged everybody, however unfit or unco-ordinated. The cons called him H, which he didn't seem to mind.

When I started weight training I could barely lift 50 pounds. Others were pumping 200 pounds repetitively. The hatred I'd stored up against all my enemies kept the adrenaline flowing. When my muscles screamed out, I reminded myself of the injustice and violence I'd received and kept pumping iron. The more it hurt, the more strength and fitness I felt I'd achieved.

During those first weeks, I was allocated a single peter on the twos very near where the senior screw resided. It was good to be on my own again. To my dismay, I was transferred from the mailbag shop to the loom shop, where they wove prison blankets on outdated looms. The mailbag screw was upset—during my two weeks there I'd become the only con he could remember who hadn't produced a mailbag.

'You've got a large chip on your shoulder, Fellowes, and someone's going to knock it off,' he said on my last day there.

'Well, I doubt if it'll be you,' I said.

By now I was embittered and didn't give a damn for anyone in authority. I'd give as much as they gave me—who dares wins.

The noise in the loom shop was deafening. The instructor showed me how to operate the loom, loading and unloading the shuttles, but I didn't want to learn. If I did, they'd keep me in that shop. My loom spent more time being fixed than actually working.

On the second day the shop screw asked me, 'How come yours is the only loom that isn't producing anything?'

'I've got no co-ordination and I'm left-handed. This is a right-handed loom, boss.'

He looked thoughtfully at the loom. 'You could be right. I never thought of that.'

'It really frustrates me, boss. I'll never be able to master it.'

He walked away pondering what I'd said. I knew I'd convinced him it was a right-handed loom.

In the middle of that week I was interviewed by the senior education officer. As he introduced the education facilities, my mind was made up. I wasn't having any of it. He talked of courses for semiliterate cons. At least I could read and write.

'Well, Fellowes, what can we offer you?'

'From what you've said, nothing.'

'That was to give you a feel of what we're doing. For you, it'd be good to build for the future.'

'What with?'

'You're an ex-policeman, so you must have a reasonable education. We can help you build on that.'

He talked about full-time education and recommended an Ordinary National Diploma in business studies.

'There's a price to pay if you go on full-time education.'

'What sort of price?' I asked.

'Because you're not producing, you'd be paid a minimum wage.'

I decided that, whatever the cost, qualifications were essential for the future.

'I'd like to take up the challenge.'

He smiled. 'You won't regret your decision, Fellowes. I'll arrange your transfer to the education block.'

I was told on the Friday I'd been accepted for the course and would start on Monday. The loom shop screw couldn't believe it.

'You've worked your ticket, Fellowes. Nobody gets in full-time education that quick.'

'They offered it and I've taken it.'

'They shouldn't allow it. Cons ought to be made to *work*.'

'It'll be better than working in this noise trap.'

The discipline screws didn't like cons being

educated; they'd have preferred making the cons work harder. The more a con suffered, the more they liked it. Most of them had been turned down by the police or fire service.

One senior screw on our wing took a dislike to me. While I was cleaning out my peter he came up and said in a loud voice, 'I hear you're going to do full-time education, Fellowes?'

'That's right.'

'Think you're a cut above the rest doing time, eh?'

'Not at all.'

'You had your chance and blew it, Fellowes.'

'What do you mean?'

'Ex-cop. You could've made a good career for yourself but you turned to crime instead.'

'Really?'

'Yeah, you're a rotten apple.'

'If you think that, it's your problem, not mine. Besides, I tried to join the prison service.'

'What happened? Failed the entrance exam?'

'No I passed all those. It was when I produced my birth certificate I failed.'

I could see he was steaming with rage, but I just smiled and walked away. In future I'd have to watch myself with him, even though I'd won the first round.

Since being in my single peter the cons either side hadn't spoken to me. It was obvious the word had been put out that I was an ex-cop. After the reception committee had done me over, the screws had kept a close eye on me. The cons couldn't get me so they ostracised me instead.

I still took care moving about the wing. Natural instinct made me aware of who was behind or beside me at any given moment. I continued to produce mental pictures of all the people I held responsible for my imprisonment. I'd dream up better ways of fulfilling the promise for revenge I'd made myself. They'd all suffer; none would escape my fanatical wrath.

The course started on the Monday morning. It was hard work at first and I had to discipline myself to concentrate. Prison isn't the best place to study, especially if you're innocent, and I sometimes lapsed into moments of remembered pain during the lectures. I'd miss what the lesson was about. Each week ended with an exam, the results being given out the following Monday. Mine weren't too impressive.

One Monday the course leader called me into his office. 'I'm concerned at your results so far, Fellowes. You're not working to your full potential.'

'I find it hard to concentrate,' I said.

'So does everyone in here, so get on with the job in hand!'

I felt disappointed and embarrassed at his comments. 'If you're going to come through,' I said to myself, 'you'll have to fight all the way and prove to people you can make it.'

From then on I worked like someone possessed, day and night. Soon I was achieving the required standard. Better still, I started enjoying the work.

There were about ten of us on the course. The others shared their understanding of subjects with each other, helping the weaker ones. They offered me nothing, and neither did the other cons on the wing. I wasn't one of them. That made me even more determined to succeed.

It was strange how the cons' catalogue of acceptance worked. Murderers, robbers, thieves and violent criminals were OK. A nonce was hated by all the cons. Police and ex-police were second only to nonces. Stranger still, the people who supported this code were often the ones most active in the homosexual stakes.

I'd see hard men and nonce-haters get all spruced up to see their wives and children. They'd return from the visiting block saying how lucky they were that their wives stuck by them. Then during the week they'd visit the wing queens to fulfil their own lusts.

They'd pay for their deviancy with tobacco, the amount depending on the services offered. As with the tobacco barons, the queens were part of another racket operated by the pimps. The screws knew it went on but never closed it down.

More horrifying was the pimps' strong-arm brigade, who'd intimidate young or weak cons to go on the game for them. One day a young con on the twos near me was visited by two pimps. I heard an angry voice say, 'We're going to have you whether you like it or not.'

A while later the young con entered my peter in tears, struggling to walk.

'What's up, Stan?' I asked.

'They've raped me.'

'What!'

'They came in, one held me down, the other raped me.'

I felt sick.

'Go to the screws, Stan.'

'I can't. They'd kill me.'

There was nothing I could do, only listen to him pour out the sordid details. He was just twenty-one and doing life. What a start to his sentence!

I lay in bed that night utterly devastated. I thought *my* life was hard, but my treatment was nothing compared to this. Prison housed some of society's worst animals. What chance did Stan have in trying to serve his sentence normally after this sort of attack? They'd all but destroyed him.

A few days later I learned the answer to my question. Stan had attacked one of his assailants with a shiv and was down in the punishment block waiting to be weighed off (tried before the governor).

Months of gym work and weight-training had made me extremely fit and strong, despite the prison diet. My reflexes were finely tuned and I could see muscle definition in every part of my body. I knew I could now handle violence if it came my way. I didn't have long to wait.

One day I was washing in the wing toilet block when two of the reception committee walked in. They started throwing cynical comments about my build to wind me up. I surveyed the toilet area—it was clear.

As I tried to leave, my right boot found itself lodged in the groin of one of them. He fell to his knees in excruciating pain. My knee connected with his head and he was out cold. The other one tried to run but I caught him by his hair and smashed his head against the wall, also giving him several heavy blows to his stomach. He finished up on top of the other con on the floor.

I grabbed both their heads and turned them to face me.

'Don't ever try to mess with me or next time you won't walk.'

The adrenaline was still flowing as I pushed my way through the gathering crowd of cons. I decided to strike while the iron was hot in case the third member of the gang planned on revenge. I ran up to the threes and found him lying on his bed.

'I've just had a meeting with your mates, and they're not feeling too well.'

He looked at me puzzled.

'Now I'm going to finish the job.'

'I don't want no trouble with you.'

That was his last remark. Then my fists engaged his head several times.

'You and your cronies come near me again and you'll live to regret it.'

Back in my peter that evening I considered my actions. I was disgusted that I'd joined the very club that had caused me so much pain and anguish. I'd met violence with violence and set myself up for some other crony who wanted to make a name for himself. All the hatred I'd stored up had been discharged in my frenzied attack. Still, I'd never made the rules of the jungle; I was just living by them.

I lay awake analysing my changing attitudes. There were numerous flaws in my character that I didn't like. Prison had encouraged and multiplied these flaws and now they were eating away all the good points of my personality and character.

The system was turning me into another of its violent conscripts. The cancer of hatred had grown out of my control. Everything I'd said to convince the system of my innocence had failed. 'You can't beat the system,' someone had said.

After much thought I decided I *could* beat it. If I were to educate myself, strengthen my body, keep out of trouble and gain the earliest possible release date, I'd have used the system to my advantage and reversed the present trend.

My decision was made. I'd take up the new blueprint for rehabilitation whatever the cost.

10 Life Inside

Christmas 1970 arrived—my first one inside. I wished myself a happy Christmas because nobody else would this year.

The atmosphere on the wings was understandably heavy. Christmas should be a time for celebration and family reunions. Every man inside Wakefield was thinking of his loved ones and the futility of his own mistakes that separated him from freedom and happiness.

The screws kept a low profile, only responding to a request to open a door or give a con a light for the one cigar he'd saved up for all year to have on Christmas Day.

The only good thing about Christmas inside were the meals. Why couldn't food be like this all year? Pet lovers gave their *animals* more nutritious food than we usually had.

I'd saved for a long time to treat myself to a couple of chocolate bars and half an ounce of tobacco. All the effort of saving was worth it for those few moments of luxury.

Christmas was a long drawn-out affair. The workshops and education block were closed until New Year, which meant cons spent eight or nine days wallowing in self-pity. Everyone breathed a sigh of relief when the holiday was over.

If Christmas was subdued, New Year's Eve was a time of merriment and excitement—another year gone and one nearer release. At the stroke of 12 the whole prison erupted. Everybody kicked their peter doors for five minutes, screaming at the top of their voices.

After the celebrations I lay on my bed and said to myself, 'Noel, this has been a hell of a year. It's gone for ever.' I turned on my mental video of the horrifying happenings and shed a few tears. 'Let's hope '71 will be a better year.'

I wrote to my parents on New Year's Day, telling them of my expectations for the coming year. Since I'd been inside my mother had written every week, sometimes twice. This was important to me. Many cons had been deserted by their families and longed for a letter from anybody.

Since my encounter with the three cons I'd been left alone and enjoyed far more security. I sensed a softening towards me from some of the others. One day a lifer stepped into my peter and asked to talk.

'Sure,' I said.

'I don't know how to say it.'

'Say it as it comes to you, Joey.'

'Well, I can't read or write and my gal's written.

138

Could you read it to me?'

I felt sad as I looked at the six-week-old letter. It had taken all that time for this poor man to ask for help. I read the letter to him four times.

'If you like, Joey, I'll write a letter back for you.'

'You won't tell anyone, will you?'

'Of course I won't, Joey.'

The next day I wrote the letter for him. My reward was in seeing excitement on his face. Within a month I was reading and writing letters for five more cons. It was a pleasure to me until I sat down to read one letter to a con and realized it was a Dear John (a letter to say she'd found someone else).

I felt a lump in my throat as I looked at the con eagerly awaiting the contents. I couldn't lie to him, but how would he take it?

'What's the matter, Noel?'

The expression on my face had given the game away.

'It's Dear John, I'm afraid.'

He looked at me. 'I'd still like to hear it.'

'You sure you're OK?'

'Yeah, man.'

I read the letter, feeling as devastated as he obviously was.

'That's it,' I said.

'She's stuck with me for six years. I've been luckier than most.'

'Maybe she regrets having sent the letter. I can write one back.'

'No, she's acted different to me on visits the past few months. Thanks anyway, Noel.'

He left under a cloud of gloom. A few days later I learned he tried to top himself by slashing his wrists with a razor blade. He was rushed to the prison hospital, but within weeks he was back on the wing.

He was one of the lucky ones. Many cons who received Dear Johns would continue to mutilate themselves year after year. To them their only escape was death, but usually they were ghosted (taken away) to a mental institution.

I continued reading and writing for others, though it interfered with my studies. After several months Joey and Chas joined the remedial classes. I'd convinced them both it would open up a whole new world. It did.

My studies were going well. The screws reminded me that, once outside, my record would nullify any qualifications. They were jealous. When they took this line I'd reply with long philosophical words. They'd storm off, knowing they'd lost the initiative.

I continued the gym and weight-training classes, with satisfying results. H took an interest in me as I pressed on in his classes. When he learnt I was an ex-cop, he showed far more interest in my well-being.

H was a fair man who always had time to listen. If the discipline screws had a con who was always in trouble, H would be given the task of knocking him into shape. He'd help redirect the con's energy into more fruitful pursuits. The few hopeless cases were transferred. If H couldn't manage them, they had to be hopeless.

I was asked to join the élite group of weight-trainers consisting of H, Ken, another instructor and a con who was the gym red band (trusty). The invitation really boosted my ego and now I got to use better equipment.

I thanked H. He just smiled and said, 'Not many can stand the pace. We'll see what you're made of.'

I rose to the challenge. Within a couple of months I'd proved my worth. The reward was that I began to know H in a more direct way than the other cons. He called me by my first name and talked about his family.

H was the first man in the system to treat me like a human being. His philosophy was simple: Everything was possible, but success depended on effort, dedication and discipline. He was in charge of every situation—the situation never controlled him. If the prison system had more people like H, it would succeed more often in rehabilitation rather than destruction.

Wakefield allowed inmates certain privileges. One was that a con could have a budgerigar in his peter. There must have been a couple of hundred feathered friends, some of them top quality birds.

When one inmate I'd read letters for was released, he gave me his pair of budgies, complete with cage and breeding box. I read all the necessary books and soon had a family of three chicks to look after.

As soon as they were old enough, I chose the strongest and most colourful chick for myself and sold the other two for an ounce of tobacco each. I named him Bobby and carried him around, tucked in my shirt. He felt secure in hearing my heartbeat.

After a couple of weeks I started training him to talk and return to his cage. Before long he'd welcome me on my return, ringing his bell and saying, 'Hello, Noel. Had a good day?'

'Sure have, Bobby,' I replied.

Soon he'd attach my reply to his question and I'd get the lot.

I sold the original pair of birds and their cage for a sum of snout (tobacco) and bought a luxury cage for Bobby. He became my close companion. Whatever my mood, he was always chirpy and happy. When I felt low as I lay on my bed, he'd fly around me a couple of times, land near my shoulder and give me his full repertoire in my ear. If that didn't work, he'd repeat the exercise until I responded.

I loved that bird. He never demanded more than to be fed. Unaffected by the pitfalls of injustice, he was happy to return to his cage whenever I commanded it.

The first-year exams were creeping up and I spent all my spare time revising. In addition to business studies, I was taking five GCE 'O' level subjects. It was a hard enough slog trying to force the material into my brain without the added handicap of imprisonment.

Studying stimulated my mind but sometimes I felt like burning my books. I'd taken on too much and the cost was too high to bear. Unlike people outside, when I felt low there was no one to encourage me. The dropout rate on the course was high because of the daily pressures and demands of prison life.

I stuck it out, and in June I sat the exams. I thought I'd failed all but one. A couple of months later I was amazed to find I'd passed business studies and four 'O' levels. The one I thought I'd passed—statistics—was the very one I failed.

At last I'd achieved something. All the endless studying had been worth it. Phase two of my plan was well on its way.

In Autumn 1971 I took up the challenge of the Open University. If the screws didn't like cons studying for 'O' levels, they absolutely hated them doing Open University. Many tried to block it. When they tried it on me, I didn't take the bait. I swallowed my pride and refused to react to the cynical comments.

I chose humanities, studying the Renaissance in art, Kafka in literature, philosophy, logic and history. We were the OU guinea-pigs in prison; there could be no dropouts or they'd close down the course.

To my surprise, I was no longer ostracized. We were pulling together as a team.

I spent my evenings reading and studying, much to Bobby's annoyance. He'd land on the edge of the book and flick the pages with his head until I acknowledged him.

One night I was studying Kafka, a jug of hot tea beside me. Bobby decided to have a drink. He perched on the edge of the jug, leant forward to take a sip—and fell in! He flew out so fast, splashing tea all over me and my books, that I rolled around my peter laughing until I cried. Then I checked him for burns—no damage at all.

During the autumn, Ken, the instructor who managed the prison soccer team, said, 'You're playing centre-half on Saturday. Let's see you perform.'

I only played for the wing team when others couldn't play.

'I'm not sure they'll accept me.'

'That's their problem, not yours. If they don't like it they needn't play.'

Ken had been groomed by H and nobody questioned his decision. We won the match and I became a regular team member. My speciality was the sliding tackle, usually taking the man as well as the ball. We played on red shingle, so my tackles always resulted in cut knees or legs. I'd wear elastic stocking covering my knees, but that only reduced injury, never stopped it.

By Christmas we were top of the league, well on course to winning the championship.

Christmas 1971 I felt worse than I had the previous year. The outside was sinking into oblivion. My memory had cleared away the past to make room for the catalogue of remembered pain, suffering and degradation it wanted to store for future use.

My wife had finally divorced me in the middle of 1971, which was understandable. But it still hurt, especially as I wouldn't see my son and daughter again. I'd only seen them once in nearly two years.

For all my wrongs during my short marriage, I loved my children. To lose them this way was the cruelest blow a father could face.

The New Year brought the usual celebrations. This time I kicked the door until my ankle was in pain. I was kicking in desperation at all that 1971 had brought me.

When the Queen's Honours list was announced that year, Joe Mounsey, head of Lancashire CID, was awarded the Queen's Police Medal, in recognition of his 'enviable crime-busting record'. The *Lancashire Evening Post* listed Mounsey's successes, including 'the Southport golf links murder, the body in the car boot murder, the Overton coin-collector manslaughter...'

In August 1972 Mounsey hit the headlines again. Blackpool police officer Gerry Richardson had been shot dead trying to catch robbers at a jewellery store. It caused public outrage. Armed with a .38 revolver, Mounsey with two other officers burst into a secret hideaway in North London and got his man again. The following March, Frederick Joseph Sewell was jailed for life—at least thirty years—and sent to Wakefield prison.

Early in 1971 I was invited to join the debating society, a team of twenty cons who debated against outside teams. It wasn't long before I was contributing to every debate.

Each debate I attended boosted my confidence and within a couple of months I was invited to be the main speaker, proposing the motion, 'This house believes in capital punishment.' Trust my luck!

After much discussion, the governor approved the motion. He doubled the screws on duty and even turned up for the debate himself.

After all I'd experienced, I didn't believe in capital punishment. But it didn't matter what you believed—the task was to win the motion. After preparing my speech for two solid weeks I felt nervous. But I launched into it with great passion and sat down 20 minutes later to rapturous applause.

To my delight, we won the motion and I was presented with my certificate. We'd defeated one of the top teams in Yorkshire and soon teams from all over the country were lining up to challenge us. The only disturbing thing was that visiting teams left at the end of debates; we returned to our peters.

With the amount of studying I was doing, my soccer training and the debating society, I was leading a very hectic life. Bobby no longer received the attention I gave him in earlier years so I decided to give him to my parents. He was fully grown and the peter was too small for his exercise.

The day of the visit I put Bobby in a small ventilated box and bade him a tearful farewell until I met him again on the outside. Despite last-minute second thoughts, I asked the visit screw to give Bobby to my parents after their visit. During the visit I spent time explaining Bobby's requirements. We said out goodbyes and I returned to my peter.

Half an hour later Brian Dodsworth, the chaplain, came to my peter. 'Noel, it's bad news.'

Instant panic set in. My parents must have been in an accident.

'It's Bobby. Your father was transferring him from the box into the cage inside the car and forgot the window was open. Bobby flew straight out.'

'Not Bobby!'

My precious friend was out there, frightened.

'What can I do, Brian?'

'I can take you around the prison and see if he's in the trees. You're the only one he'll respond to.'

I spent a long time with Brian walking the prison walls but there was no sign. I returned to my peter absolutely distraught. That night I spent hours looking out of my small window, wondering where he was. It was cold and he was probably desperately trying to find his way back to me.

Most of that night I walked my peter in tears. I didn't eat anything for two days. I couldn't get Bobby out of my mind.

Other cons tried to comfort me with gifts of tobacco and condolences. My dad wrote explaining what had happened. Reading between the lines, both my parents were deeply upset. I wrote back saying it was an unfortunate accident and not to blame themselves.

It took a long time to get used to the fact that Bobby wasn't around any more. While studying I'd look round, expecting to see Bobby pecking at my books or examining my tobacco, but he wasn't there.

In Wakefield I spared little thought for my former police colleagues in Morecambe. But in early 1972 they had a clever success.

Travelling villain Lenny Pilot, one of the three to rob the wages office in Warsop Town Hall (Chapter 8), had decided to rob an optician's. Pilot and an accomplice attacked Harry Wooliscroft and took £8 from the till. They split up but Pilot was seen in a Morecambe cafe and arrested. On 21 March he appeared before local magistrates.

Pilot tried a sob story, saying the other man had said he knew where work could be found. 'Before I knew what had happened he took [the money] out of the till and the owner came.'

The story didn't convince the jury. He was jailed for six months for theft and causing actual bodily harm.

Easter brought the usual soccer competition, with the finals played on Easter Monday. We faced the might of B wing in the final. As always, the cons had put all the tobacco on B wing to win.

Our strategy was to take out one of their star players early in the game. Ten minutes into the game, I took out their centre-forward with a sliding tackle. I was booked for the offence, while the centre-forward limped off with grazed knees.

We won 2-1 after a fierce battle. I was returning to the wings to celebrate our historic victory when I heard a voice say, 'You cost me eight ounces of snout, you filthy pig.'

I looked up to see a sock filled with a snooker ball descending in my direction. I felt the impact on my head and fell back down the stairs.

When I came round, most of the team were there. They carried me to have a cold shower, which returned me to the land of the living. I knew my injury was serious as blood was pouring from my head.

'How bad is it?' I asked.

'You've got a gash about two inches long.'

'Who the hell did it?'

'A lifer from A wing who lost his snout.'

'He'll lose more than his snout when I get my hands on him.'

'It's been taken care of. The screws have got him.'

My head was aching and I felt dizzy as I stood up. The screw said I'd have to go to sickbay, then make a statement.

'I'm all right. I slipped on the stairs.'

'Everybody saw what happened. Now it's time to get your own back on that maniac before he kills somebody,' said the screw.

'Not me, boss. I don't remember anything.'

'Very well, Fellowes. If you want to be a hero, we can't make you.'

I had a few stitches and returned to my peter. The con who'd sprung me faced the governor and received a few days down the block and loss of earnings. He asked for protection because he owed the barons so much. The barons' peters were raided and he was ghosted to another prison.

Wakefield housed some of the UK's top criminals. Arthur Hosein, who allegedly helped kill Muriel McKay, the wife of a newspaper magnate, was my hairdresser. He always protested his innocence. Unlike the prison barber, Arthur had a natural talent for cutting hair.

Most notorious criminals had been given the label by the press. Inside they got on with their bird like the rest of us. To the professional criminals, bird was nothing more than an inconvenient interlude in their prosperous careers. They all shared a common hate of cops and ex-cops so, except for Arthur, I steered well clear of them.

I fell into depression again. Days seemed to get longer and the nightly torment of nightmares got worse. When I'd wake up, my bed would be wet with sweat and my lungs gasping for breath.

Eventually I spoke about it to Brian Dodsworth, the chaplain. All the cons trusted Brian because he was a man of principle and deep conviction. If he believed in something, he'd fight for you to the bitter end. At the same time, he spared no words in pointing out lies and deceit.

He saw me a couple of days later and suggested a second job to take me out of the intensity of my studies.

'What sort of job?'

'My red band's leaving me soon and I'd like you to take his place.'

'What about my studies?'

'The work of a red band's minimal. You could easily do both.'

'I've only done a couple of years. Usually red bands are nearing the end of their sentence.'

'I choose who I want to work for me. If I want someone, I make sure I get him.'

A couple of weeks later I collected my red band —worn around the upper part of the right arm. With it came a host of privileges. I could walk round the prison unaccompanied and didn't have to be banged up for lunch or supper. Not that I took advantage of the privilege at first; I feared an attack on me.

My duties included cleaning Brian's office, running messages, making coffee for visitors and preparing for church services. The only drawback was working on Sundays. The church was used for showing feature films twice a week. Half the prison saw the film on Friday night, the other half Sunday night. Cleaning up afterwards was a laborious job.

It was an escape from the noisy atmosphere of the main prison, a place of silence and solitude where I could relax in complete safety. I'd take my books sometimes and complete my essays. There was nothing spiritual about my time there. Back at the trial I'd decided God wasn't a reality. My philosophy was 'I think, therefore I am'.

Midweek Brian ran Bible studies for cons who were Christians and I'd make coffee for them. The holy joes resented the fact that I was Brian's red band rather than one of them.

I respected Brian's faith and trust in me. The feeling was mutual, but I did break his trust in one small way.

On certain Sundays I'd prepare communion— wafer biscuits and wine. I'd drink half a bottle of the wine, then fill it up with water, knowing they wouldn't notice the difference. The holy joes would be on their knees taking bread and wine and I'd look on, knowing it was watered-down. They might get parole but they weren't getting their wine!

I built up a good relationship with Brian. Now I had two people I related to—Brian and H. Both had different qualities but similar goals. They were two men desperately fighting the tide of archaic rules, regulations and procedures.

Brian had been right. The dual role of working and studying had taken away the monotony and replaced it with balance and purpose. It was then that a third person entered my catalogue of acceptable people—Eric Treacy, the Bishop of Wakefield.

He visited the prison every two weeks on a Saturday morning, sharing breakfast with the cons before his informal chats in the church. He'd always bring his wife, affectionately known as Aunt May. They both took an interest in cons and their family circumstances. In fact, May used to take cons' families overnight and feed them.

The Bish would open up the talk after breakfast with current affairs and everyone was encouraged to take part. He always made sure the less articulate had their say. Another attraction was that the Bish always brought a couple of packets of cigarettes, which he passed round.

Many stories were told in prison about the Bish. He'd step in to help cons in trouble. He'd demand to see the cons in the punishment block if he heard a whisper about the screw having beaten someone up. Without Brian or the Bish, many more cons would have suffered under the hands of the punishment block screws.

The Bish always headed the Christmas and Easter services. To him, prison offered the true meaning of those celebrations unspoilt by commercialism.

One day, just before the usual Saturday morning meeting, I saw Aunt May sitting with her eyes closed, praying softly.

'You look happy when you're here,' I said when she'd finished.

'I'm always happy when I visit this church.'

'Why's that? There's nothing but bad news around this place.'

'Well, Noel, in all the churches I've visited in the world, this is the one where I feel God's presence greatest. Considering Wakefield's history and all the poor men who've been hanged or served life sentences here, there's been a lot of prayer offered to my God. I just know he's here.'

I believed her. That short conversation never left me. I didn't experience God while I swept the church or sat to study. I just accepted that the Bish and Aunt May were genuine, caring people.

My case was due before the parole board in mid-1972 and I hoped my case would be approved. The parole officer explained that reports on my attitude and behaviour, together with facts about my conviction and sentence, would be presented to the board. They would then recommend their findings to the Home Secretary, who'd decide whether or not to grant parole.

'Have you anything to say about your conviction, Fellowes?'

'I'm innocent. Nothing's changed.'

'You're still denying the offence?'

'Absolutely.'

I came away despondent. I'd only been questioned for 10 minutes; the normal time was half an hour.

The second interview was with the shrink. If you've been convicted of killing, the shrink makes an independent report to the board.

'I see you're still protesting your innocence,' he said.

'Absolutely right.'

'The minute you accept your guilt, Fellowes, the better your life will be.'

A real Catch-22 situation.

'If you keep me here to the last minute of my seven-year sentence, so be it. I won't admit to something I've never done, nor will I ever give up my fight to clear my name.'

'Fair enough, but we have to be sure of people we recommend for parole.'

'I understand.'

'Look at the size of you—six-foot-two, weighing 210 pounds. I sure wouldn't like to meet you in a dark alley.'

Then I blew it. 'I'd sure like to meet *you*,' I said.

With that, the interview finished. My chance for

parole was lost. I'd shown no remorse for the killing I'd never done. Bitterness flooded back and, with it, depression.

Many cons who'd done several years were on sleeping draughts to calm them down. I'd see them outside the sickbay every night, waiting for their daily tot. They'd drink the tot in front of the medical screw, then leave through the exit door.

Once outside, they'd spit out their tot into a cup. After collecting five or six tots, one of the cons would drink the drug cocktail. They'd each get a turn. To see the recipient staggering around the wing, bombed out of his brain, was a very sorry sight.

I was called to see the assistant governor one lunchtime.

'811168, Fellowes, sir.'

'Well, Fellowes, it's not good news. Your application for parole's been refused.'

I'd expected it, but I still felt disappointed.

'It's not surprising, Fellowes. You're still denying the offence and besides, several people have written in saying they fear for themselves if you're released.'

'Who are they, sir?'

'That's confidential. It's not unusual. Many are frightened of the person they spoke against at his trial. Keep your nose clean—there's always next year.'

I returned to my peter angry. Who were these faceless people? They were right to be frightened. If I got my hands on them it'd be a long time before they could write again.

The shock of the board's refusal sent me into a frantic rage. I started kicking everything and shouting abuse at the top of my voice.

After 20 minutes I fell on my bed exhausted. My peter looked as though a bomb had hit it. My knuckles and feet were throbbing after using the peter door as a punchbag. At least I'd vented my anger on objects, not people.

For days I felt low. One lunchtime a member of my letter-reading group noticed.

'You look really down, Noel. Had some bad news?'

'Yeah.'

'What's up?'

I explained.

'What you need is a pick-me-up.'

He returned with a home-rolled cigarette.

'There you are. Smoke that.'

'I've got snout of my own. What's the big deal?'

'It's full of dope, man. It'll take you out of yourself.'

Drugs, including dope (marijuana) and acid (LSD), were widely available in Wakefield. Wives or girlfriends would put them in silver paper or a condom, keeping it in their mouths and transferring it with the welcome kiss. The con would swallow the package. Once back at his peter he'd drink glasses of salt water to vomit it up.

I smoked the joint, which left me floating on a cloud. Gone was the anger. Colours seemed more vibrant and periodically I'd burst into uncontrollable laughter.

The effects lasted well into the night and left me with a famine-type hunger. The next morning I devoured everything at breakfast, which was unusual for me.

Dope was definitely an escape out of the reality of prison life. The drawback was that once I'd come out of its influence, the reality of my situation hit me with a vengeance.

I continued to smoke dope occasionally throughout the rest of my sentence. The few hours' release it gave were worth the down times I endured after its influence. I was lucky—it never cost me a bean. Unlike others, I never advanced to other drugs on the black market.

It was exam time. Open University had been a long, hard slog and now was the time to put another year's study to the test. The exams were gruelling and we all knew failure would result in the authorities closing the OU door for us.

The fateful day of the results arrived and Dennis Nash, the course leader, came into the study room with a beaming smile.

'You've done it, lads. You've done it.'

Ninety per cent pass rate, myself included. I enrolled for another year and decided to do a couple of GCE 'A' levels, too. After all, I still had plenty of time to kill.

I was also pleased that two cons I'd encouraged to go to remedial classes had completed a year and were continuing with their classes this year. Both had a real appetite for learning. At least their new reading and writing skills would help them go straight once they were back in society again.

Christmas 1972. My third in prison. 'How many more before they'll release me?' I thought.

My only contact with the outside world was when my parents, brothers and sisters visited me. The visits had become less frequent. My mother used to write frequently asking me to send a visiting order. But the longer my sentence ran, the more difficult visits became. I'd make excuses for not sending one.

My peter door opened and in walked Brian.

'Happy Christmas, Noel.'

'Happy Christmas to you, Brian.'

I notice he was clasping a small carrier bag.

'I've brought you a couple of things to thank you for all your efforts since you've worked for me.'

'Thanks.'

'Don't tell anyone, or I'll find myself in real hot water.'

'I understand, Brian.'

He left and I examined the contents—biscuits, tinned meat, savoury snacks, coffee, evaporated milk and candy. What a surprise! To think that Brian had put his job on the line just to give me a better Christmas. The very thought brought tears to my eyes.

It was in keeping with Brian's beliefs and it showed me something about the true meaning of Christmas. That evening I had a private feast, eating food I hadn't tasted in years.

As I prepared the church for Christmas Day communion I decided never again to drink the wine and then water it down. Brian deserved better.

The New Year brought ice and snow for quite a long period. Soccer matches were cancelled and we spent several weekends locked in the main prison. Tension approached breaking point and there were several fights. Even the screws were pleased when the weather finally broke.

At Easter we again won through to the soccer final, to be played against our old enemy, B wing. During the first half it was obvious they wanted a physical game as off-the-ball fouls started to wind players up and tempers started to flare.

H stopped the game at one point and told both captains that if the game didn't clean up he'd abandon the tournament and cancel all future competitions.

The second half got under way and the score was still 0-0. When a high ball was kicked, I decided it was mine, leaping up to head it. I noticed two opposing players coming for the ball. My head connected with the ball but their heads connected with my nose. A loud crack rang in my ears and I was awash with blood.

As I lay on the ground, I heard one say, 'That's done you, cop. It should've been your neck.'

H came over, wrapped a towel over my face and then examined me.

'The game's over for you, Noel. It'll need an operation to fix that nose.'

'Is it bad, H?'

'I'm afraid so.'

'I can't lose face, H. I'll have to finish the match.'

'OK, but don't even *try* to head the ball.'

The player who'd done the damage was sent off and we eventually won 1-0.

The whole of my face ached. After showering I looked in the mirror. My nose had been spread all over my face and already two black eyes were appearing. In the sickbay I was given painkillers and told that I'd see the doctor in the morning.

It was a restless night as the pain grew more intense. The mirror reflected a mass of bruising to my eyes, nose and lips.

The doctor arrived at the sickbay and examined me for about 30 seconds.

'This man needs an operation immediately.'

'How bad is it, doc?' I asked.

'Quite serious. Your nose has been badly smashed and we need to fix it right away.'

The surgeon at the prison hospital saw me that afternoon.

'I'll arrange for an operation tomorrow morning at Pinderfield Hospital. Don't worry, it'll look as good as new when I've finished.'

The following day I was escorted to Pinderfield Hospital, dressed in prison uniform and hand-cuffed to two screws. It was embarrassing to see the public quickly move out of our way as we walked the long hospital corridors. Goodness knows who they thought I was—some arch-villain, no doubt. My face didn't help and when we arrived at the annex the nurses looked positively frightened.

1 Noel Fellowes as PC 1289 Fellowes in 1968.

2 Mrs Hockenhull, Harold Parkinson's daily help.
3 Detective Chief Superintendent Mounsey, who led the 1970 investigation into Harold Parkinson's death.
4 Harold Parkinson with his famed coin collection.

5 The murder room on 26 February 1970, the day Harold Parkinson's body was discovered.
6 Noel Fellowes in 1985 stands on the steps of Lancaster Castle. He was dragged up these steps barefoot in the winter of 1970 to be charged before the magistrates.
7 Mr Justice Caulfield, the judge at Noel Fellowes' trial in June 1970.

8 The 'missing' taxi-driver record sheets for Noel Fellowes on 24 and 25 February 1970. It was alleged in the trial that Noel had stolen the sheets to cover his movements at the time Parkinson was killed. But the 1984 investigation turned up the records among the papers on the case.

9 *(Top)* HM Prison Wakefield in West Yorkshire. Noel Fellowes spent most of his sentence here.
10 *(Left)* A typical prison cell at the time of Fellowes' imprisonment.
11 *(Above)* Joe Berry, who travelled to Overton with Billy Clark on the night Parkinson was killed.

12 Detective Chief Superintendent Bill Lumsden who headed the initial 1984 enquiry into the Overton killing.
13 Deputy Chief Constable Eric Evans ran the full-scale enquiry on the case in 1984.
14 Detective Chief Inspectors Tom Eyres (left) and Allan Potts (right) re-investigated the killing. Potts had proved himself earlier by obtaining Billy Clark's confession.

15 *(Top)* Fourteen years later, Noel Fellowes visits the house in which Harold Parkinson was killed. Noel said, 'As God is my judge, I have never stepped through that door before today.'
16 *(Left)* The Lord Chief Justice, Lord Lane.
17 Bob Westerdale, the *Lancashire Evening Post* crime reporter, who brought Noel Fellowes the news that the case was to be re-opened in 1984.

18 Noel and Coral Fellowes, after Noel was vindicated from any involvement in the crime, outside the Appeal Court on 12 July 1985.

The screws took off the cuffs and I donned the white operating gown I'd been given. A couple of nurses returned to give me a premedication injection. They were shaking.

As they approached the bed I said, 'Boo!'

They jumped back, startled, and I laughed.

'Don't worry, girls. He's one of our better lodgers,' said the screw. 'Come on, Fellowes, behave yourself. There aren't many cons who get this sort of day-trip.'

'OK, boss.'

After my jab I was wheeled to the operating theatre and again met the surgeon.

'This won't take long. You'll soon be back to normal.'

'I doubt I'll ever be that again!'

The next thing I knew was a female voice saying, 'Mr Fellowes, wake up.'

I was fighting to breathe and felt heavy weights on my body. When I opened my eyes I realized that two nurses and four screws were sitting on top of me.

They all jumped off and the screw explained that I'd reacted in a violent way to coming out of the anaesthetic, kicking and flailing my fists about.

An hour later I was on my way back to prison, where I stayed in the prison hospital for a week.

'It's a great success,' the surgeon said when he examined me. 'Take it easy for a month and you won't notice the difference.'

I thanked him for his speedy help. H came to see me in hospital and cracked a few jokes about my looks. He also said that if I didn't get out soon he'd have to find a replacement for weight training. Typical of H—always the motivator.

Before long I was back on the wing again. I'd lost study time, and exams were only a few weeks away. It was a case of literally burning the midnight oil. The lights went out at nine but I used candles. Brian had given me permission to take the altar candles when they were no longer of use, which was when they were three-quarters of the way down.

Just before exams began I was informed that my annual application for parole had come up. I told Brian I'd decided not to apply, but he encouraged me to try as I had nothing to lose. I applied and met the parole board man.

'This is your second application, Mr Fellowes. Has anything changed?'

'Nothing other than spending another year inside and having my nose broken again.'

'Well, we've got all we need from our last interview. What about your attitude to the people you say put you into this position?'

'My hands are tied. I still hold them responsible, but I have no intention of revenge. I live in the hope that one day my name'll be cleared. Besides, I'm planning to start a new life in Bracknell, 250 miles from Morecambe. There's nothing apart from hurt in the memory of Morecambe.'

'Very well. That's all.'

Returning to the wing I felt as before—no chance.

Exam time came and again I passed. After three years I felt weary of studying and needed a break. H invited me to become red band for the gym. Brian was reluctant to see me go but said if I really wanted to, I could. It was a difficult decision because I respected both men.

My transfer approved, I started working for H and loved it. I became friendly with him, telling him of my past and my plans for the future. He advised me of situations to avoid once outside again.

I became superfit and one of the strongest weight-trainers in prison. H advised me not to seek revenge against the con who'd broken my nose. In Wake-field gym red band was the best number. I wasn't going to risk my job for a few minutes of revenge.

Christmas came. If I kept myself out of trouble, I had just 10 more months to go before my earliest release date of November 1974.

In January I was called to the assistant governor's office.

'811168 Fellowes, sir.'

'Well, Fellowes, you'll be pleased to know your application for parole's been approved. You'll be released on parole on 25 January.'

'What?'

'You heard right. 25 January you're going out.'

I was speechless. Fifteen days and I'd be out.

Back in my peter I jumped up and down on my bed like a boy who'd just opened his Christmas presents. I'd done the system out of 10 months inside! Brian and H were delighted with the news.

I had final interviews with social and welfare officers, including a long list of dos and don'ts. I was told I was eligible for a set of under-clothes, socks, shoes, a jacket and a pair of trousers.

I chose the best of the old-fashioned clothes on offer and waited for the final day of my imprisonment to end.

11 First Taste of Freedom

I awoke on 24 January, 1974 excited that tomorrow would bring the ultimate answer—freedom!

I had a mixture of excitement and apprehension as I thought of life outside these cold, grey walls of captivity. In nearly four years I'd hardly made a decision. Everything had been thought out for me. Soon I'd have to make decisions again. Would I be up to it?

The earlier encounters with violence and intimidation had left scars in my attitude and personality. I'd become intense, hiding behind a mask of extrovert behaviour. Behind the façade was a frightened, insecure man, fighting for reality and recognition. To survive in prison I'd had to live by the unwritten rules. In society, the rules would be different and I'd long since forgotten them.

In the last four years I'd viewed society through glossy magazines—new houses, stylish clothes, beautiful women. Was this reality or a toyland of my imagination? Only time would answer this question.

In 24 hours from now, I'd start to find out.

I spent most of the day saying goodbye to Brian, H and the other acquaintances I'd shared my life with. There were discharge formalities and at lunchtime I had a final meeting with the governor.

'811168 Fellowes, sir.' There was a hidden satisfaction in the words. Tomorrow I'd be a person again, not a number in a primitive penal institution.

'Well, Fellowes, your final day under our care is drawing to an end. I hope you've learned well and make a useful contribution to society in your future.'

'I intend to do my best, sir.'

'Many faces pass through Wakefield, Fellowes, but you've used your time productively. I wish you well for the future.'

'Thank you, governor.'

He probably gave the same line to all the cons who were due for release, but at least they were words of encouragement.

In the afternoon I tried on my new clothes. I felt like a million dollars. Everything fitted perfectly. The mirror reflected a new person. Gone was the drab prison clothing. I was looking at a tall, well-dressed man I hadn't seen in years. I dropped the tailor red band half an ounce of snout for doing such a good job, then went back to the wing.

It was time for the tradition of distributing my excess belongings to the cons who'd served me best. At Joey's peter I dropped off my radio and jacket, then took my sports gear and reading material to Geordie's. They were both pleased.

My peter was bare. Just a bed, slop bucket, wash bowl and jug. After all the wheeling and dealing over the years to acquire luxuries, I'd disposed of them in five minutes.

After the meal I spent my last evening on association. Playing table-tennis seemed a good way of killing time, taking my mind off the dreaded clock. But I was so excited that I was thrashed out of sight! The cons laughed their heads off. They knew what I was going through. The last few hours are always the worst.

At 8.30 the bell went. The peter door was slammed shut by the discipline screw.

'Best of luck on the outside, Fellowes.'

'Thanks, boss.'

I lay there for hours trying to sleep. In the end I counted sheep but after reaching 600 I gave that idea up. I must have dropped off because I woke to the sound of my peter door opening.

'Come on, lad. You don't want to be late for your release, do you?'

I leapt out of bed, my stomach turning over and my legs like jelly.

'I'm going home. I'm actually going home,' I said to myself over and over. I remembered my arrest and initial remand. The feelings were similar, but this time I had everything to look forward to.

Within a couple of minutes I was on my way to reception. As I passed Joey's peter I kicked the door.

'See you, Joey,' I shouted.

A load of abuse came from the other peters, where cons were trying to sleep.

'See you, lad,' shouted Joey.

'See you suckers again sometime,' I shouted.

Another load of abuse came flooding back. I carried on walking, laughing at the more colourful remarks.

'Keep your comments down,' said the screw to me in an angry voice.

'OK, boss.'

At reception I changed into my new clothes. Now I'd be able to wear what I wanted. The reception screw checked my belongings. All I had was a box of letters from my mother and my exam certificates.

The time was 7.10. I was to be released at exactly 7.30.

Another screw asked me to sign a form and handed me £18—my entitlement on release. Not bad for four years' work! I felt like throwing it back at him. What a paltry sum to build a new life on! I felt sad for anybody leaving Wakefield having no family or friends to rely on. What chance would they have on the outside with £18?

The clock struck 7.30 and the screw ushered me to the picket door inside the main prison gatehouse.

'Your time's up, Fellowes. Off you go.'

The door opened and I stepped into freedom. Tears formed in my eyes as I saw my mother and dad waiting in their car.

I walked slowly towards the car, then stopped and looked at the prison for the first time from the outside. Anger welled up as I surveyed the walls and cell-blocks. Wiping away the tears I vowed that no one would ever imprison me again for something I hadn't done.

My mother greeted me with a hug and a kiss. My dad seemed lost for words, but his face said it all. They were both thrilled.

Within minutes we were out of Wakefield and heading south on the motorway. My dad looked tired.

'What was the journey like coming up, Dad?'

'We hit everything possible—snow, ice, fog. We set off at two this morning and at one stage we didn't think we'd get here on time. When the weather cleared 80 miles away, I put my foot down and was stopped by the police for speeding.'

My heart sank. 'What did you do, Dad?'

'I told the officer we were coming to pick you up from prison at 7.30. We were concerned that you'd be released and we wouldn't be there to meet you.'

'What did he do?'

'He believed me and let us go.'

At least there were still police who had credibility. We talked about family and other day-to-day things. Then a new anxiety crept over me. We were travelling at 70 miles an hour along a motorway; the fastest I'd travelled in four years was at running pace. The sheer speed of the car and the traffic heading in the same direction frightened me.

The further we went the more anxious I became. I closed my eyes and gripped the door handle tightly, hoping we'd stop soon. My mother noticed and worked out the reason for my silence and sweating. She offered a comforting hand.

'I'm all right, Mother. I'll soon get used to it.'

Much to my relief we stopped at a service station. I'd survived the first 60 miles.

'Let's get some real food,' my dad said as we walked to the service area. I felt excited at the prospect of choosing what I felt like eating.

My first full English breakfast went down a treat. It was the best breakfast I'd tasted in my whole life. We continued our journey and by the end of the motorway I was beginning to relax.

In the early afternoon we arrived in Bracknell, where I intended to build a new life. As we drove through the town, I told myself, 'This is it, Noel. New town, new life and new chance to make something of yourself.'

I surveyed my parents' house from the car and it finally sunk in—I was home. Only hours ago I was in my peter; now I was home. The very thought blew my mind.

Once inside, the first thing that struck me was the size. It seemed so dark and tiny. Wakefield held 600 cons; this held five people. I'd imagined it to be much bigger and lighter from what I'd seen in the magazines.

My brother Paul and youngest brother Roger were still living at home. My other brother, John, had married while I was serving time. Kay, my youngest sister, was a nurse living in Windsor.

Roger arrived home from work. He was warm and sincere in his welcome towards me. When Paul arrived he seemed edgy. I sensed apprehension as I went to hug him. He backed off and I realized he was still carrying guilt at what had happened in court four years ago.

I knew the truth: He'd been a mere pawn sacrificed in the game to destroy me and still he carried the guilt.

'I'm really pleased to be home again with you, Paul,' I said.

'So am I.'

Those few words took the intensity out of the situ-ation. We ate dinner together and chatted about family news. Then Roger offered to take me shopping the next afternoon. I accepted. It'd be good to see Bracknell centre and I still had the £18 to spend.

My first night of freedom was spent watching TV. The doors were kept shut to keep the heat in. Every time someone left or entered the room, they shut the doors. I got up to open them again, just a fraction, so I could see they were ajar.

As I watched TV, I kept waiting for the bell to indicate it was bedtime. Ten o'clock came and, exhausted, I went to bed. Clean sheets and a comfortable mattress—sheer luxury.

In bed I lay soaking up the memorable day. It all seemed a dream. I felt so contented and happy. I didn't want it to end in case I woke up in prison again.

The next morning, my fears were realized. I woke up in strange surroundings—curtains, wallpaper and a strange room. I panicked, then, with relief, realized I was home.

Downstairs my mother was cooking my breakfast. The others had left for work. My probation officer arrived at midday—a friendly woman who asked about my first impression of freedom and my plans for the future.

She told me there were no restrictions other than having to report to her office once a week to chat over the way things were going. I'd imagined parole meant far more restrictions.

Thirty minutes later she was on her way.

'Thanks, Mrs . . . .'

'Norma. You can call me Norma.'

'Thanks, Norma.'

Roger returned at one o'clock and, after a quick bite to eat, we went shopping in Bracknell.

As we arrived at the multistorey car park, Roger handed me £30. He'd only just qualified as a butcher and he'd saved his money for me!

'I can't take that, Roger.'

'Honestly, Noel, take it or I'll be offended.'

'What can I say, Roger? Thank you. I'll never forget it.'

We walked through some of the larger stores and I felt everyone was looking at me. I bought trousers and a shirt. Paying for them was another hurdle. While I was inside, the currency had gone metric and I had to fumble in my pockets to come up with the right amount. I was given my change—coins I'd never seen before. Roger explained their value. Another lesson learned.

After an hour I felt weary. Everything moved slowly in prison, yet outside people rushed to and fro.

'I'll have to go home, Roger. It's all too fast for me.'

'OK.'

Back in the security of home, I reflected on the shopping trip. The simple task of buying clothes had revealed my deep inferiority and insecurity. I'd felt embarrassed at trying to pay for the clothes and—even worse—speaking to the lady behind the counter.

Could I ever adjust to it? For the time being I felt better off at home. Both Paul and Roger invited me out in the evenings that followed; I declined, making excuses as best I could.

The following week I started a job as a labourer on a building site in Paddington, London. My dad was the site agent and I was working for him.

When we arrived at the site, my father introduced me to the other labourers. The contract was to demolish a large house and build luxury apartments in its place. I was given a sledgehammer and told to knock down internal walls.

During the morning some of the men started asking probing questions.

'How long have you been home?'

'Why did you come from the north?'

'Are you on the run?'

My defence mechanism sprang into action. I told them it was a trial period in the south.

'It's all right for you,' said one Cockney. 'Your bleedin' old man's the gaffer. He'll look after you.'

I knew they thought I was a soft number so I

worked twice as hard. By the end of the week I'd won their respect. The years of weight-training had paid off. Now they accepted me as one of the boys.

Another boost—my first wage in four years. The packet revealed a staggering £60, a small fortune to me. The money I'd earned was mine. After giving housekeeping to my mother, I went to my bedroom and counted the money over and over, like a child counting his piggy-bank savings. I decided to save and buy a whole new wardrobe of clothes.

After work on Monday I had to report to Norma at the probation office. Trying to cover my real feelings, I told her that everything was going well.

'How are you adjusting to everyday life?'

'No problems at all.'

'That's remarkable, considering your time inside.'

'Well, obviously, I have to make minor adjustments, but generally things are good.'

'Are you getting out much?'

'Occasionally with my brothers, but that suits me.'

'Good. See you next week.'

I was relieved. Norma was a lovely lady, but to me she belonged to the system. I didn't trust anybody other than myself and four years on my own had reinforced that belief. The less the system knew about me, the more I liked it.

During further weekly visits I learned to answer her questions in a way that flattered her. My cunning was still intact. Her training had been formal and calculated; mine was gained at grass roots.

The trouble with the system is that it punishes the individual through the deprivation of prison life, then tries to rebuild him from scratch. The logical thing would be to do the rebuilding right from the start of the sentence, not after release.

After I'd spent two weeks at home every evening, Roger asked me to go out with him. I reluctantly accepted and went with him to a local pub. To my surprise I enjoyed myself. The place was packed and the opposite sex was much in abundance.

Two ladies drew us into conversation. I hadn't talked with females for a long time.

'Where do you come from?' one asked.

'Wakefield.'

'Where's that?'

'Yorkshire.'

'Want to buy me a drink?'

'Why? Haven't you got any money?'

She laughed. 'That's a new one.'

'OK. What you drinking?'

'Gin and tonic, please.'

I returned with half a lager.

'Sorry. Didn't have enough money for the gin and tonic.'

'You really *are* cheeky, aren't you?'

'Yep, I sure am.' There was no way I was going to spend my hard-earned money on someone else's pleasure.

We continued talking, but the smell of perfume coming from her direction sent my legs wobbly. The sweet fragrance of femininity had long since been replaced by male sweat and slop-out buckets. She was giving me the come-on.

It was a good job Roger was there, keeping his eye on me.

'Nice to have met you, but we've got to go,' I said.

Relief covered Roger's face. We made our way out, but she continued to follow.

'Aren't you going to ask me out?'

'Can't afford it.'

'OK. I'll see you here at seven on Sunday.'

Satisfied, she returned to the pub and we went home. I had no intention of showing up. Women weren't in my plan just yet.

The following week my dad asked if I wanted to ease back into driving again.

'I'm not sure if I could handle the speed and the traffic.'

'If you don't try you won't find out.'

The plan was that I'd drive to work early in the morning when there wasn't much traffic on the road. I nervously sat in the driver's seat, started the car and off we went. It felt strange and at the first junction I panicked and stalled the engine.

'It's no good, Dad.'

'You can do it, son. Start her up again.'

At the next junction I stopped perfectly.

'Take your time. Adjust the speed to your confidence.'

After 20 miles I felt as though I'd never stopped driving. He was right—to win, you had to try. I drove to work every morning for a week or two, growing in confidence.

One afternoon my dad said, 'You can drive home tonight, if you like.'

This was my big test—driving through London at the start of the rush hour. I rose to the challenge and drove home without a hitch. Now I could drive anywhere on my own.

Life was sweet. I had a job, money, a secure home and, most of all, my freedom. My confidence was growing and I was learning to cope with people and situations every day.

One Sunday evening I decided to go down the road for a quiet drink by myself for the first time. My parents seemed happy at the idea. Off I strolled to the Golden Farmer pub and ordered my pint of lager.

As I sat minding my own business, a man appeared at the bar, about thirty-five years old, medium build and around five-foot-seven inches tall.

'Give me a whisky, Jimmy,' he shouted. As he waited he looked me up and down angrily. Trouble! I could sense it a mile away.

Drink in hand he came up to me. 'See you, big 'un. I don't like yer.'

'You don't even know me.'

'I don't like yer and that's it.'

'Look, I don't want any trouble. I'm just having a quiet drink.'

'I'll give yer trouble, big 'un.'

Then he walked away.

'Take no notice of him,' the barman said. 'He's aggressive in drink. Any more trouble and I'll order him out.'

'OK.'

I decided to drink up and go. But before I could finish, the mad Scotsman returned.

'How about you and me, then, big 'un?'

'Sorry, mate. I don't want trouble. You better find someone else.'

I knocked my cigarettes on to the floor on purpose, then stooped down as if to recover them. I looked him straight in the eye, then grabbed his private parts and squeezed them as tightly as I could. Instant pain reflected on his face, his mouth opened wide and a deep groaning emerged.

I kept a tight grip for 30 seconds and, when I saw his eyes starting to roll, I let go. He fell into a crumpled heap on the floor, gasping for breath.

'I told you I didn't want any trouble.'

I doubt if he heard me. People in the bar hadn't even noticed what had happened. I swiftly drank the rest of my lager and left.

Luckily, it was my first visit to the pub. Nobody knew me there. In future I'd have to give it a wide berth. It was just my luck—out on my own for the first time and ending up in trouble.

At home my mother asked if I was all right.

'Everything's great,' I said.

Little did she know that I was sweating with anxiety in case the police should come knocking at the door. An hour later I began to relax again. After that incident I decided in future to go out at night only in my brothers' company.

The first month of freedom had involved unlearning prison life and routine. I'd coped well but remained introverted, only speaking when spoken to. I lived with the nightmares of the past and knew I had to protect my new-found anonymity, no matter what the cost.

Since my arrival at home neither my parents nor brothers had mentioned prison or the case against me. I wasn't too concerned, but it meant I had to lock all my hurt and frustration deeper inside myself. At least I had a family and a home to return to.

One of the men at work offered to sell me his old car for £50. After close examination of the Ford Zephyr, I decided to buy it with my savings. I was now the proud owner of a two-tone car—white and rust. It wasn't the classiest car, but it was reliable. Roger helped me fill the holes, which occupied my time in the evenings.

Norma, my probation officer, was delighted with progress and extended our meetings to once every two weeks. I was relieved as I always clammed up at the probation office—it reminded me of my recent past.

Paul was engaged to a girl called Linda in Reading and seemed to spend most of his time over there. I wondered if he wasn't too pleased at my being home, but Roger assured me it was his normal lifestyle.

One Friday Paul asked me if I'd give him a hand over the weekend to finish off a garage he was building for a friend.

'It's good money, Noel.'

On Saturday I went with him to work. It was the first chance we'd had time to talk for any length of time. He told me about his forthcoming marriage to Linda and the need for extra money to cover the wedding expenses.

'I'm really pleased for you, Paul.'

'Thanks, Noel. You'll never know how much I love Linda.'

'Listen, Paul. I need to put a couple of things straight. Since I got home you've been uneasy with me. I want you to know that I never blamed you for giving evidence at the trial. The police must have put the frighteners on you, saying you committed the crime with me and I was covering up for you.'

'Absolutely right. They scared me to death, wrote out a statement and told me to sign it. Then in court I told them I hadn't done a number of things and the barrister twisted what I said.'

'Well, stop worrying. Both you and I know the truth.'

'I just can't forgive myself, Noel. It really haunts me all the time.'

'Paul, I really love you as a brother. You know that, don't you?'

'Yes.'

'Then stop carrying this burden. It doesn't belong to you.'

'I'll try.'

We worked together all day and I could see he was more relaxed than I'd seen him since my release. By six o'clock on Sunday evening we'd finished the job and shared the money. Feeling exhausted, we headed home in Paul's car.

'I just want to stop at the Three Frogs and tell Linda I'll see her later. OK?'

'Sure. No problem.'

The Three Frogs was a pub in Wokingham where Linda worked part-time. Paul went in to see her and I stayed in the car. A couple of minutes later he returned.

'Linda wants to meet you, Noel. Come in for a quick drink.'

'I can't go in there in my working clothes.'

'Course you can. It's all right.'

'OK.'

Once inside, Paul introduced me to Linda. When Linda had served our drinks I noticed a lady walking towards me. She had striking red hair.

'Coral?'

'Yes, Paul,' she said in a cultured voice.

'This is my older brother, Noel.'

'Pleased to meet you,' I said.

'Where've you come from?' she asked.

'We've been building a garage down the road.'

Coral smiled, her whole face lighting up.

'I didn't mean that, silly legs. You haven't got a southern accent, have you?'

'I've just moved down from the north. We'd better make tracks or our dinner'll be ruined.'

Both Linda and Coral said goodbye and we left.

'What do you think of my girl, then?'

'She's nice.'

'What about Coral?'

'The sort of woman dreams are made of—sheer class.'

'You can say that again.'

'Sheer class. Sheer class.'

We both burst out laughing. The funny thing was, I really meant what I'd said.

12 A Remarkable Woman

In mid-March 1974 the weather changed for the better—spring was in the air. I was looking forward to the long days.

Nearly three months had passed since my release, yet it felt like yesterday. Although I was free, the torment of prison lived on in my dreams every night.

Much of the past was still locked within me. I never shared the horror of my nightly fears with anyone; nobody would understand.

One evening Paul came in from work.

'Remember Coral?' he asked me.

'The one with the red hair and big smile?'

'Yeah. She really fancies you.'

'I don't believe you.'

'No kidding, Noel. Here's her phone number. She'd like you to give her a ring.'

Paul passed me the piece of paper with the number on it.

'I can't ring her up. I don't even know her.'

'She's expecting you to call and ask her out for a drink. That's all you have to do.'

'I wouldn't know what to say to her.'

'Would you feel better coming out with Linda and me? We could make a foursome.'

'That'd be a good idea.'

'OK, arrange it for Friday at 7.30 and we'll all go out together.'

Within 10 minutes Paul had gone again. I paced the hallway excitedly, trying to think how to open the conversation. I desperately wanted to make the call but inherent insecurity prevented me.

After 15 minutes I dialled the number and the ringing tone sent me into a cold sweat.

'Who's speaking?' asked a warm, inviting voice.

'I'd like to speak to Coral.'

'This is Coral.'

My legs turned to jelly.

'Er—this is Noel, Paul's brother.'

'Hi, Noel. What can I do for you?'

'Well—er—I was wondering if you'd like to come out for a drink next Friday, along with Paul and Linda.'

'Where to?'

I didn't have a clue.

'It's a surprise,' I said, relieved at the sudden idea.

'OK. What time do you want to pick me up?'

'About 7.30.'

'Fine.'

'Thanks,' I said as I put the phone down. I couldn't believe she'd said yes. Then I realized I'd forgotten to ask where she lived!

I was really excited at the prospect of taking Coral out. The big day arrived and, heart in mouth, I phoned Coral, asking her where she lived.

'I was expecting you to call,' she said. 'I thought, "How can he pick me up when he never asked where I lived?"'

I felt a fool. What on earth did Coral think of me?

We drove to Coral's house. To my surprise, a teenage girl opened the door.

'Does Coral live here?'

'Mum, it's a man for you,' she shouted.

'Ask him in.'

I stood in the hallway confused.

Coral came downstairs looking stunning.

'Sorry to keep you. I had to make sure the baby was settled.'

Had I heard right—a baby?

'This is Danielle, my eldest daughter.'

'Hi, Danielle. Pleased to meet you.'

We left to join Paul and Linda. My mind was working overtime. Was she married? Divorced? Single parent?

We arrived at Boulters Lock restaurant near Maidenhead. It was a classy place. Drinks in hand, Coral and I wandered on to the terrace overlooking the River Thames.

'Tell me about your children, Coral.'

'I've got three daughters—Danielle, Louise and Olivia. Their father went off with another woman when I was seven months pregnant with Olivia. We're divorced.'

'I feel desperately sorry for you, Coral. It must be

hard for you and your girls coping with the impact of it all.'

'We're happier without him. At times it's difficult financially, but it's all worth it really.'

I detected a defence barrier going up so I pitched in with my own marriage break-up, leaving out the interim years in prison. We talked about love, marriage and relationships with mixed emotions for nearly an hour.

Coral was a great listener. I opened up to her as if I'd known her for years. We'd both suffered injustice in our past. Hence the openness.

Paul popped his head out of the door. 'If you don't come in you'll freeze to death.'

We'd been too engrossed to notice the cold.

'Just coming, Paul.'

'You two seem to have a lot to talk about,' said Paul as we joined him and Linda in the bar.

'Just talking about past experiences.'

'Good. Now you're back, let's order a table and have a meal.'

His request surprised me.

'Can I have a word, Paul?'

He made an excuse. In the toilets I said, 'You told me we were going for a drink, not a meal.'

'I thought as you were having such a good time with Coral, a meal would be in order.'

'It's my first date and I haven't got enough on me to buy a meal.'

'I've got enough, and down here it's normal to take girls out for a meal.'

'How much will it cost me?'

'With the wine about £20.'

'No way,' I retorted.

'OK, if that's how you feel.'

We returned to find the girls missing. As they returned to the table, they both started laughing.

'What's so funny, Linda?' asked Paul.

With that they burst into more laughter.

'We went to the ladies' and they must back on to the mens'. We heard everything you two talked about.'

That appealed to my humour and I burst out laughing.

'Forgive me, I'm still adjusting to the southern way of life. I give in—let's order a meal.'

'Honestly, Noel, I'm quite happy not to eat,' said Coral.

'Coral, I'm really sorry. It's such a wonderful evening. Let's finish it in style and eat.'

Following a superb meal we dropped Coral off at her home and she invited me in for coffee. I declined.

'Perhaps I'll see you in the Three Frogs sometime?' she said.

'I look forward to that.'

It was well after midnight when I arrived home. It had been a wonderful evening. Coral had broken through my sophisticated defences and opened up past hurts and feelings.

For the first time in years I'd spoken my true feelings about my ex-wife. My son and daughter were at the forefront of my thoughts daily and Coral was the first person I'd talked to about them.

Despite having experienced violence in her past and desertion while carrying a child, she was stable and secure. What a remarkable woman—warm, loving, understanding, mature, caring, gentle! I was introverted, insecure, embittered, aggressive and broken. The more I saw of Coral the more I'd truly learn about myself.

On Sunday evening I went to the Three Frogs half an hour before closing time. Coral welcomed me with a beaming smile.

'I was hoping you'd come and see me.'

'The pleasure's mine,' I said.

After Coral finished serving drinks, we returned to her house.

'Why do you work at the Three Frogs?'

'Since my divorce I've needed to meet people without any ties. Besides, you don't get medals for wallowing in self-pity.'

'I'm sure you're right.'

'Also, living on social security doesn't keep us in the lifestyle we're used to. Working a couple of evenings a week gives me the maximum I'm allowed to earn while on benefits.'

She was growing in stature with every sentence.

'What made you phone me for a date?' she asked.

I related the conversation Paul and I had had. She laughed.

'What's so funny?'

'Only that Paul said *you* fancied *me* and wanted to take me out. I told him you'd have to ask me yourself.'

'So we were both set up by Paul!'

'We sure were.'

'It was worth it. Without Paul I might never have met you. I really enjoy your company.'

'The feeling's mutual.'

That last remark set my heart fluttering. It was an unfamiliar feeling. After several deep breaths I said, 'Could I take you out again, Coral?'

There was a short pause.

'I'd like that, but I must make sure the children are happy.'

'There's no rush.'

'Perhaps you'd come round and spend an evening here?'

'Fine.'

On Sunday Coral invited me to the evening meal. I arrived mid-afternoon feeling nervous in case the children didn't like me.

Danielle was a confident, mature fourteen-year-old. Louise was a shy, quiet ten-year-old with striking blonde hair. She kept her head down as we were introduced. It was obvious she'd been the one most affected by her father's leaving. Olivia was a bouncy two-year-old with huge eyes, totally loved and spoilt by her big sisters.

After the meal I played with the children. Olivia loved every minute of it; Louise, on the other hand, remained polite and courteous but I could sense her insecurity. I felt happy in their company.

After a couple of weeks the children began to warm to me. Although I barely knew them, I'd really become fond of them all. Every time I visited Coral I sensed real love and peace in the house. It was a family scene I'd never set eyes on before.

I was falling in love with Coral. We complemented each other and I lived for the evenings when I could see her again.

A month after the start of the relationship I knew I couldn't carry on with it in deceit. Coral had been open and honest with me, but I still hadn't told her about the killing I'd been convicted of. Would she reject me? I decided to tell her the truth. I wouldn't be able to cope with the emotional upheaval of rejection later.

That night in her lounge she detected something was troubling me.

'You're quiet tonight, Noel. What's wrong?'

'There's something I need to talk to you about.'

My heart beat faster and the insecurity from my past caught up with me.

'You know I care for you, Coral.'

'Yes.'

'The truth is, I've fallen in love with you and there's something in my past I haven't told you about.'

'Well, go on.'

I related the whole story in every detail. It took the best part of an hour. I kept looking for a glimpse of her reaction, but she showed no hint of surprise or emotion.

'Well, now you have the story of my life, what do you think?'

She just looked at me, her face expressionless.

'If you say you didn't do it, Noel, I believe you.'

She actually believed me! Someone I'd known a month actually *believed* me. All the torment and worry had gone; Coral knew the truth. The tension of the last hour vanished into thin air.

'How does this affect our relationship, Coral? I'll understand if you don't want to see me any more.'

'It doesn't make a bit of difference. You've told the truth and I believe you. Seeing you've been so open, I need to tell *you* something.'

'This is turning into confession time.'

We both laughed.

'I just want you to know that I love you.'

To hear that she loved me was beyond my wildest dreams. Tears formed as we embraced.

'This is the happiest day of my life,' I whispered in Coral's ear.

'It's not been a bad day for me, either.'

After that, life was sweeter than I ever imagined it could be. Coral had given me hope and purpose for the future. I lived to please her and her children.

Having worked for a few months, I now felt I could look for a better job in the Bracknell area. I'd given up the idea of showing employers my educational qualifications because they'd then know where I'd obtained them.

I managed to get a job with Expandite, travelling all over southern England sealing expansion joints in buildings and bridges. They gave a basic wage with lucrative bonuses and as much overtime as I wanted.

Within a couple of months I was earning top money. The disadvantage was working away most of the time and only seeing Coral at weekends. I'd phone her at least four times a day and send her telegrams. If nothing else, being away from Coral during the week proved my love for her.

One Friday night after returning home, I changed and rushed round to Coral's. Louise answered the door and we started chatting.

A voice called down the stairs. 'Is that you, Daddy?'

Taken by surprise I replied, 'Yes, it's me.'

Olivia said, 'I knew I had a daddy.'

Coral came down after settling Olivia for the night. She explained that Olivia had been playing with some neighbouring children. They were all standing in a line waiting a turn on the slide. One of the older boys said only children with daddies could have a turn so Olivia couldn't have one. The poor child had run home heartbroken.

From that day on Olivia always called me Daddy. When I came home I spent all my time with Coral and the girls. We fitted into each other's lives perfectly.

In between coffee, cuddles and kisses one night, I said, 'Coral, will you marry me?'

'Of course I will.'

We told the children about our engagement over a special dinner party the day before my birthday in September 1974.

'We've got a very special announcement to make. Your mother and I are engaged, and with your approval we're getting married next September.'

The children cheered and clapped. After the

initial excitement, Louise said, 'Does that mean I'll be able to call you Dad?'

Her remark really touched me.

'If you want to call me Dad you certainly can.'

'That'll be great.'

The girls spent the rest of the evening making wedding plans.

Coral and I arranged my birthday party and invited both sets of parents.

Halfway through the party I stopped the music and announced our engagement. You could have heard a pin drop.

Rosa, Coral's mother, said, 'You shouldn't joke about things like that, Noel.'

'It's true,' said Coral. 'We're getting married a year from today.'

The place erupted. Everyone was delighted. The children took great pleasure in telling everyone that *they'd* known the day before. It made them feel special.

Coral and I, together with the girls, drew up the wedding plans. Being in love suited me. Coral had brought real purpose and balance into my life. She introduced me to her friends and when they asked questions about my past she'd step in and cover for me admirably.

In those early months of trying to re-establish myself, Joe Mounsey, the man who'd put me behind bars, continued his career development.

In September 1974 he went to the scene of a post office killing in Accrington, Lancashire. Derek Astin, a former Royal Marine, had bravely attacked a masked intruder but was shot dead. Mounsey immediately linked the crime with a similar raid in Harrogate, Yorkshire—clearly the work of the notorious Black Panther.

Mounsey ordered checks on 2000 shotguns in Accrington and made plans to interview every man in the town. He saw the crime as a personal challenge and later hosted a conference of senior detectives involved in the Panther hunt. Mounsey was one of the few officers in the case not selected for criticism when the Black Panther, Donald Neilson, was eventually cornered in December 1975.

Neilson, a 29-year-old former soldier, planned every crime with military precision. When he was arrested in Nottinghamshire, their chief constable barred all other forces from the initial interviews. But Joe Mounsey, keen as mustard, tried to meet him. Mounsey's investigation had unearthed more than enough evidence to put him away for life—one of five he received at Oxford Crown Court in July 1976.

A vacancy arose for a contract supervisor's job and I was interviewed by the managing director, Bill Dolan, a Welshman.

He told me I'd performed well.

'You're not the average sort of person who takes on this kind of work. Do you have any qualifications?'

'Just a few "O" levels and an OND Business Studies certificate.'

'I *thought* you'd been educated.'

I felt uncomfortable. He was definitely percep-
tive.

'Well, Noel, I'm offering you the position of contract supervisor, with a salary, company car and
expenses. If you prove yourself after 12 months, I'll
consider promoting you to contract surveyor.'

'How long do I have to consider your offer, Mr
Dolan?'

'Give me your answer by Monday morning.'

I left his office jubilant. When I told Coral the
news she was overjoyed. Although it meant an initial drop in salary, it was a chance to start climbing
the management ladder. If Coral believed I could
succeed, that was good enough for me.

I gladly accepted the post. Within a few months I
had the workforce going at full speed to get good
monthly results.

The new job meant I was home more often and
Coral and I could see more of each other. But it was
obvious that my salary and Coral's family allowance
wouldn't meet the weekly outgoings once we were
married.

'We have each other and together we can
manage anything,' she told me.

As usual she was positive and confident in me.
I only hoped I could live up to her expectations. I
wanted Coral to have the wedding she desired so
I supplemented my income by taking on building
work in the evenings and at weekends. To my
relief, a couple of weeks before the wedding I'd
reached my financial goal.

But having worked 14 hours a day during the week and 12 a day at weekends, I was drained. Pride had been my downfall. People had offered financial help with the wedding but I'd refused as I wanted to meet the costs myself. I'd always found it easy to give but impossible to receive.

I'd been best man at Paul and Linda's wedding a year earlier, so I asked Paul to do the honours for me. My younger brothers, John and Roger, agreed to be ushers.

On 27 September, 1975 Coral and I were married at the Methodist church in Bracknell. All our hopes and plans came together in a single moment as we looked each other in the eyes and said, 'I will.'

Louise and Olivia stood next to us in their bridesmaids' outfits, tears of joy streaming down their faces. Love had found a way for *them* as well. I loved Coral and the children so much it hurt.

I spent the early months of our marriage learning to live with four females, adjusting to being a husband and father. Coral and the girls had been used to making decisions themselves; now I was being asked to make family decisions. I didn't even know the rules of family life, let alone the answers.

Coral again was supportive, constantly encouraging me to take the lead.

In early 1976 there was purpose and balance flowing through the family. Financially we were only just keeping our heads above water, and I saw it as my responsibility to provide for my family.

The pressure eased when I was promoted to contract surveyor. It meant more money and an annual bonus measured on performance. My primary objective was to achieve better results than the others. A number had tried to stab me in the back, metaphorically speaking, but I'd served my apprenticeship in Wakefield Prison and recognized their knives before they'd even drawn them.

My desire to succeed became an obsession. I'd always earned respect as a supervisor, but now I cracked down on the troublemakers and within a couple of months they sought different employment. Now I had the right team for success.

I was still fearful that someone would learn the truth about my past and I'd be out on my ear. Promotion had both fed my ego and made me more defensive. I viewed every question directed at my past with suspicion, and I'd counter them with rhetoric.

My nightmares got worse, becoming violent and horrifying. I'd wake from them sweating and shaking. Coral asked what they were about but I didn't want to worry her with them. The result of all this was deep insecurity, a bout of black moods and depression.

After very bad nightmares I'd wake in the morning physically and mentally exhausted. Coral knew the signs and tried to reach me with words of comfort and understanding. But my depressed state had to run its course. When I returned to normality I'd feel guilty, as Coral and the girls were always the ones who suffered.

It was worse for the children. To them I was just in a mood, silent. Coral always protected me by saying I wasn't feeling well and would recover soon. It was heartbreaking to see the four people I loved most in my life suffer because of past injustice I'd suffered. It made me even more bitter against the system.

In September 1977 a photo appeared in the newspaper of a man with bushy grey hair and black-rimmed glasses. Dr Alan Clift, the forensic scientist who'd spent so long in the witness-box at my trial, had been suspended from his job while police probed his work.

Assault charges against three men were dropped on the orders of the Director of Public Prosecutions, following scrutiny of Clift's work.

In June 1981, truck driver John Preece appeared before appeal judges after serving eight years of a life sentence for murder. The judges ruled that Clift had been discredited 'not only as a scientist but as a witness'. Preece was freed and later received a record £77,000 compensation.

A 50-year-old man was freed from a mental hospital after six years following the court testimony of Clift.

Geoffrey Maycock, jailed in 1968 for raping and killing an 84-year-old spinster, was cleared. Fibres from the scene of the murder and those found on Maycock's clothes played an important part in the case. But Clift's evidence was 'not up to the standard required for a criminal trial'.

The Home Office Criminal Department was working overtime to see whether there were more miscarriages of justice in over 1500 cases handled by Clift.

'There was evidence of bias, carelessness, inaccuracy and a failure to have kept abreast of modern scientific work,' according to the findings of a Home Office report on Clift published in the *Observer*. 'He does not seem to have turned his mind to the possibilities of his evidence incriminating people, trusting that the police were always right in their initial suspicions.'

After leaving the service, Clift reportedly went into publishing and book-keeping. He had apparently received nearly £50,000 in salary and expenses during his term of suspension.

Success at work for me meant sacrificing family life. In my new job I often had to be away from home. There's a fine line between working for a living and living for work. In Coral's view my attitude to my work was shutting the door on our relationship and our life together as a family.

When the chips were down I knew that my love for Coral and the children was far greater than anything else. We agreed a policy that I'd work whatever hours were necessary during the week and devote the weekend to the children.

By the end of 1977 anyone viewing my life from the outside would see a reasonably successful manager, happily married, living on a secure salary. It was all a mask. Having worked flat out for months,

I was exhausted. To counter the increasing night-mares I was staying up until the early hours so that I'd sleep soundly. I'd wrestle with the reality of my existence during the hours I was alone downstairs.

I had everything any man could ask for, yet I wasn't fulfilled. I concluded that the reason lay in a package in the dungeon of my mind labelled 'injustice'. Coral tried everything to break through my defences, but I couldn't bring myself to share the horror of it all.

As always, Coral would smile and say, 'Don't worry. I still love you.'

If she'd said it once, she'd said it a hundred times. I doubted if anyone other than Coral could have put up with me and my constant swings of mood.

She was everything to me. All I had to do was try to be everything to her. Surely love would find a way.

13 Search for Truth

1978 arrived to the sound of singing, dancing and cheering on my part. I was in a drunken stupor following hours of heavy drinking.

The alcohol had taken effect. My head and body refused to respond to the simplest of commands and I finished up in a heap on the floor.

I'd really let myself go. All the frustration of 1977 had been drowned in beer and whisky.

'It'll all be better this year, Coral, I promise.'

'You've had too much to drink, Noel.'

'Wait and see. It'll be our year.'

'I wish you'd stop drinking, Noel. You'll pay for it tomorrow with a lousy hangover.'

Coral was right. Whenever I drank too much, I paid for it the next day. So did the family. Drinking was my escape from reality. The problem was it cost more and more money to achieve the required effect.

Once the alcohol had worn off, I was left to face mental stress, anguish and remembered pain, as well as guilt at having acted irresponsibly towards

Coral and the family. I concluded that this was my destiny—a life filled with inner hatred, bitterness, anger, frustration and fear.

The one element of my life that seemed to be prospering was my career. Since starting the new job at Evode I'd attained promotion and a fat bonus for target achievement. This enabled us to buy our house. When the price was finally agreed, however, we didn't have enough for the deposit and legal fees. Rosa and Brian, Coral's parents, offered to lend us the balance until my next bonus was due.

Coral was delighted at owning a house but I had reservations about having to find a mortgage payment every month as well as settling the loan from my father-in-law. It was yet another pressure, and our living standard dropped.

I was spending sleepless nights worrying about finances. Now I regularly dreamt I was dead, which led to deeper bouts of depression and longer periods of isolation.

My brother John was visiting us more than I thought necessary. He was heavily into Christianity. Unlike Roger, who was also a Christian, John couldn't stop talking about Jesus, God and his beliefs.

I'd convinced myself that God didn't exist following my prayer in the sweat-box at Lancaster Assizes back in 1970. Now the mere mention of Jesus or God sent me into fits of rage. While I respected my brothers' beliefs and admired their lifestyles, I didn't want any part of it.

One Sunday morning Coral told me she was going to church with my brother John.

I knew she'd been under tremendous strain because of my moods, so I said, 'If that's what you want, you go.'

Underneath my response, I was seething with rage. If they thought Coral was going to be another Jesus freak, they had another think coming.

I challenged Coral after she'd been a second time.

'Why are you going to church all of a sudden?'

'I don't know. It gives me time to think things over.'

'What things?'

'Just things personal to me.'

There's no way I want you to become a Jesus freak.'

'I don't think I would.'

I made sure. Each Sunday I arranged to visit relatives or go to the beach.

Everything seemed back to normal until Coral and I had an evening meal with Paul and Linda. After the meal I was a little merry to say the least. Back at Paul and Linda's house my parents, who'd been baby-sitting, asked how the evening had gone.

'Plenty of food, booze and jokes,' I said, 'so all in all a great night.'

Coral and I stayed for a nightcap with my parents.

Suddenly my mother asked, 'How are you, son?'

'I've already told you, I'm fine.'

'I know you said you're fine, but how do you *really* feel?'

'He's still having trouble sleeping,' said Coral.

'The nightmares are worse and now I keep dreaming I'm dead. It's really tiresome,' I quipped.

She looked at me carefully. 'I think God's telling you you're spiritually dead, Noel.'

'Don't give me that heavy religious stuff, Mother.'

'I really believe it's true.'

'I can't handle all this Jesus stuff. Besides, they're just bad dreams recalling past hurts.'

But my mother continued. She believed God was speaking into my life. I knew my mother had been a devout Christian since as far back as I could remember. I tried to trip her up about her beliefs but she just answered every question I threw at her.

She seemed peaceful and secure. It was the first time I'd listened to her real beliefs. Coral and I were engrossed.

'It's four o'clock,' Paul declared.

'It can't be,' I said.

We'd been talking about God and my dreams for four hours.

I spent the next few days thinking over what we'd talked about. It was fine for my mother but not for me. There was no real proof that God existed at all.

A couple of weeks later on a Saturday afternoon the doorbell rang and my brother John stood there, looking pale and nervous.

'I've come on what should have been a long journey, but was a short journey.'

'Stop talking in parables, John, and tell me what's wrong.'

He reached inside his coat and produced a book.

'I felt I had to give you this.'

He held out a Bible.

'Put it on the table, then.'

I was just relieved to hear that there was nothing wrong with his family.

'You mean I can leave it here?'

'It's only a book, John. What's the big deal?'

'Nothing. It's just that when God tells you to do something and you do it, it gives you purpose and joy.'

The colour had returned to his face and he was beaming.

'Why are you so happy, John?'

'Normally you'd have been aggressive towards me at the mere mention of God, but this time you haven't reacted.'

'You been speaking to our mother lately?'

'No, I haven't seen her for two or three weeks.'

'You haven't heard anything about my dreams?'

'Honestly, Noel, all I know is that God told me to bring that Bible round and I was scared stiff.'

I knew he was telling the truth.

'I believe you. Thanks for the book.'

He left with a smile on his face and a spring in his step. John and Gillian had struggled financially since their marriage. But whatever their circumstances, they always had a sense of security and peace.

Coral and I talked about John's sudden visit. I decided he was trying to get us to church. Coral said that if there was a God perhaps he was trying to speak to me.

'Rubbish. You're starting to sound like one of them already.'

'Well, like it or not, that's what I think.'

I gave Coral the benefit of the doubt and put the Bible on my bedside table. Over the next few days, that Bible seemed to stare me in the face every time I entered the bedroom. A week later I noticed it was missing.

'Coral,' I shouted. 'What's happened to my Bible?'

'You're never going to read that, so I put it in the wardrobe.'

'Yeah, OK.'

I went to the wardrobe, rescued it and opened the Bible for the first time. It fell open to Isaiah Chapter 53. I read the chapter through twice, closed the Bible and thought about what I'd read. It didn't make much sense but I felt the need to read more.

Over the next week I read a little of the Bible each day, hoping to find the answer to my problems. I didn't see or hear God, but something was definitely happening—I had a new desire to seek the truth.

Towards the end of September my youngest brother Roger called to see us.

'Have you spoken to John lately?' I asked.

'I saw John and Gill last week. Why?'

'I thought John might have mentioned about his message from God.'

'About bringing you a Bible?'

'So you know about all that?'

'Yeah, John told me.'

I explained to Roger what had happened over the last few months—the talk with my mother, John bringing the Bible and the dreams I was still having.

'What do you make of it?'

'I really believe God's speaking to you in a big way.'

'How come all of you are hearing him and I'm not?'

'If you're serious about meeting God, Noel, he'll meet you.'

'I'm serious all right. I've got quite a few questions to ask him!' I said angrily.

'He'll meet you, if you really want him to.'

'Where is he, then?'

'God's alive and well in a church in Bracknell.'

'Which church?'

'I'm not telling you. If you mean what you say, go and find him.'

'A game of hide-and-seek, is it?'

'It's not a game—it's reality.'

Very shrewd, my younger brother. He knew I'd rise to the challenge of trying to disprove God.

'I might give it a go.'

'It's your choice, Noel.'

The next Sunday Coral and I took Olivia to our local church to meet God. It was terrible. We came home laughing at ourselves for going there in the first place. But we decided to take up the challenge and visit other churches in the town over the next few weeks. Even if we didn't find God, it'd be good for a laugh.

After visiting three or four churches, I was convinced God was a figment of Christians' imagination. There was more life in a graveyard than in some of the churches we visited.

A couple of weeks later Roger came to see us.

'You conned us, you liar. We've been all round Bracknell looking for God. He isn't there and doesn't exist.'

'He's alive and well. That's the truth.'

'I don't want to hear any more of that crap, Roger. Anyway, where do *you* go to church?'

'Bracknell Baptist Church.'

'You better watch out. I might turn up and tell people what you are,' I joked.

'You're more than welcome any time.'

I talked it over with Coral and we decided to go to Roger's church. What did we have to lose? It was the very last church I was going to, anyway. On the last Sunday in October, off we went, Olivia in tow.

We arrived to excited talking, people greeting each other with hugs and kisses. Everyone seemed so pleased to be there.

I turned to Coral. 'These are definitely weirdos. Keep your eyes open.'

Coral smiled. 'Let's wait and see what happens.'

We took our seats in the centre row. The minister, Ben Davies, stood at the front with some other men. As he prayed simply over the meeting, I detected a pure Welsh accent. He boldly spoke about God, then asked us all to stand.

As the people started to sing, I couldn't believe it! People were clapping and playing tambourines. The place shook to the sound of people rejoicing. Everybody seemed on a high. Perhaps it was pumped-up emotion? It was certainly different from anything I'd seen before.

At the start of the next song, I found myself gripped in muscular spasm. I could see and hear, but every muscle was locked. I tried to move my head or speak to attract Coral's attention, but I couldn't.

Then what can only be described as a heat fell on me. It came in through the top of my head, spread over my entire body and went out through my toes. Over and over again it continued to flow through me.

After what seemed like an eternity, but which was probably only about a minute, I felt the hurt I'd carried for so many years coming out of my stomach. I stood there, tears streaming down my face, unable to control them.

As the hurt came out, peace started to fill my whole body. I knew I'd met God in a very special way. I kept saying in my head, 'Thank you. Thank you.' I knew I'd met the living God.

The heat left just as suddenly as it had come and my body was able to respond once again. I collapsed on the chair saying, 'Oh, God. Oh, God.'

I turned to Coral. There were tears on her cheeks. The singing stopped and she sat down. I was shaking like a leaf.

I leaned over to Coral and said, 'I've just met God.'

'I know.'

I didn't hear the rest of the service. I just kept reliving what had happened. It felt wonderful.

On the way out Ben Davies stopped me. 'You're Roger's brother, aren't you?'

'Yes, I am.'

'You've just become a Christian, I hear.'

I thought, 'This is unbelievable. The man knows what's happened to me.'

'No, definitely not me.'

'Really?'

'Yeah, but something happened and I need to talk to you. I met God today.'

'Incredible. How about coming to see me on Wednesday evening?'

'It'd be my pleasure.'

Coral and I arrived home full of everything that had happened. I felt very different. There was a peace and security in my life that God had planted deep within me. My life had completely changed. Even better, Coral had met God at the same time and in the same place.

Wednesday came and Coral and I poured out to Ben everything that had happened on Sunday. Then I told my whole story—the case, arrest, prison, new life. Ben was transfixed.

'What do you think of that lot, Ben? Any chance for me?'

'Jesus'll sort everything out for you. As far as I'm concerned, if you say you didn't do it, mate, then I believe you.'

Now I had two people who knew about the case and believed in my innocence. Something had been released inside me to enable the hurt and locked-up frustration to come out.

Ben talked about a new life to be found in Jesus. We could be brought back to God through Jesus Christ by being reborn spiritually. The only way was to repent—turn away from our selfish lives—and trust Jesus, serving him with our lives.

I'd heard the 'born-again' label but thought it was a new cult, not something to do with Christianity.

After meeting God in such a tremendous way on Sunday, we were totally convinced. Ben joined us as we talked to God, turning away from our past wrongs and asking Jesus to take control of our lives.

It was over in minutes. Once more a heat poured through me as I spoke out the words to God. I felt clean and secure. There was peace, joy, reality, purpose, love—all flowing through my life. Everything seemed wonderful and perfect. I felt completely new.

Coral and I shed a few tears. We felt privileged enjoying God's love together. Since Sunday our lives had changed. My face beamed with happiness. Coral's, too. In fact, she'd been smiling for so long I thought it'd become a permanent feature.

Later that evening, I phoned the whole family to tell them the news—my mother, John, Roger and my sister Carole. They were thrilled. They said they'd been praying for Coral and me for several months.

Carole said, 'Prayer changes things. Isn't God good, Noel?'

'He's great.'

The following week everybody noticed my happiness. I told them I'd met God in a dramatic way and now I was a Christian.

'Jesus lives in me,' I said.

They were surprised, especially as before I'd been so opposed to religion. Now there was no stopping me telling everyone I spoke to.

Each night Coral and I read the Bible together. We couldn't get enough of it. One night we decided to pray together so we knelt down on one side of the bed, hands together in prayer-like fashion and stared at each other.

'What do we say?'

'I don't know.'

'Let's just talk to God, then.'

'Sounds OK to me.'

We talked to God about everything on our minds. I asked him to show the whole world I was innocent. At the same time, I wasn't sure if we were allowed to ask God for things. But I knew he loved me so I reckoned it must be all right. There seemed so much we didn't know.

Before long, Coral and I joined a 'foundation course' at church, aimed at new Christians. Within a couple of months we'd learned much more about how to pray, and the Bible came alive to us. We were thrilled to learn how much God loved and cared for us.

Louise and Olivia became Christians. So did Coral's mother, my dad, my brother Paul and many others. So many of our prayers were being answered that we kept wondering if we'd had our portion already! We experienced Jesus' love day after day, month after month.

In early 1979, a couple of months after being born

again, we were baptized in a huge tank of water and became members of the church.

The week following our baptisms I was driving to London listening to a tape of worship songs, joining in and thanking God for all he was doing in my life. Suddenly my voice changed as I started to speak in a strange language. I felt frightened. It went on for a couple of minutes and then I started talking normally again.

I turned the car around immediately and headed home. I needed to tell Coral what had happened. We prayed about it, asking God to reveal the truth about the experience.

The same evening I was in the bath and it came on me again. This time I decided to get help, so I phoned one of our ministers, Alan Marshall, and explained what had happened.

He came straight round and asked to hear the whole story again.

'You've been baptized in the Holy Spirit, Noel.'

'Wow! I knew it was something different.'

This new experience was a gift called 'speaking in tongues'—a special language given to a Christian by the Holy Spirit to use for prayer and worship.

Alan and I then prayed with Coral and she received the Holy Spirit and spoke in tongues as well. This experience brought a new dimension to our lives and we became even more aware of God's presence in our daily lives.

My life had changed dramatically, but some of the old problems were still there.

My big struggle was with forgiveness. God wanted me to forgive my enemies, but I just couldn't. I forgave with my lips but my heart held bitterness and resentment. I desperately wanted to obey God, yet I failed in so many ways. The more I tried to conquer wrong in my life, the more I failed. It seemed impossible to be perfect.

I was helped by one of the church elders, Maurice Robinson, who was also our family doctor. He gave me some wise counsel.

'Let God wash through your life, Noel, instead of trying to do all the work yourself. Let the Holy Spirit reveal areas of your life that need changing. Relax. God's in charge.'

Maurice was right. I'd kept falling short of *my* standards. My standards and God's were completely different. He knew I could and would fall from time to time.

I hadn't grasped how much God had forgiven me. The time I spent with Maurice was the first of many times over the following years, each meeting resulting in more change in my life.

Slowly things started working out. My anger subsided, as did swearing, cursing and a memory for crude jokes. It seemed small stuff but at least I was moving in the right direction.

In mid-November 1979 I answered the door to two men with northern accents.

'Noel Fellowes?'

'That's me.'

'We're police officers investigating a murder in Shap, Cumbria. We'd like to ask you some questions.'

A man had been found bound up; he'd died from his injuries. It was similar to the killing I'd been convicted of in 1970.

'Shap's 300 miles from here. Why are you asking *me* about it?'

'We're just eliminating suspects.'

I shook with fear. Everything the police had done to me in 1970 came flooding back. But Coral was able to verify what we'd been doing on the night in question and they left, satisfied at my alibi.

It took me hours to get back to normal. I wrestled in prayer over the following months about it. It was all very well being assured that God was with me, but I wanted *action*. I wanted my name cleared.

In 1980 I learned of Ian Andrews, a man with a gift of healing from God. I phoned him up, told him of my past life and asked if he could help me. He said he'd pray about it and if he got any answers he'd ring me back.

I felt despondent. How could I untangle the past if no one helped me understand how God's healing worked? Since the visit from the police my life had been up one week and down the next.

A week later Ian Andrews phoned me back and invited us to his home in Somerset for the day. I was excited, hoping to find all the answers and come home free from the remembered pain.

We arrived at Ian and Rosemary's and, after coffee, Ian and I got on with the business.

Ian asked me to tell him everything—hurts, fears, anxieties, relationships, injustice—the lot. I poured my heart out all day. After long deliberation Ian spoke.

'It's quite simple, Noel. You need to be healed from anger, resentment, bitterness, rejection and an orphan spirit.'

'How?'

'All we need do is ask God the Father, and he'll do it.'

As Ian prayed I felt God's hand on me, releasing me from inner turmoil and tension. A new peace welled up. I felt clean all over.

It was as if I was bathing in the ocean, the tide lapping over my body continually.

My emotions had been unlocked and in the following months I was able to be absolutely open with Coral. For the first time in our marriage we had genuine communication. Our marriage took off. Gone was the heaviness that had hung over our relationship. Love flowed—sharing, caring and encouraging each other.

Since our encounter with Ian and Rosemary, we wanted to know more about God's healing and other gifts God gives his people. We felt the time had come to leave the church and join a local Christian fellowship which was partly under the spiritual leadership of Ian Andrews. Ben Davies was sorry to see us go but wished us well.

I felt sad at leaving the place where Coral and I had been shown tremendous hospitality, understanding, support and encouragement. The one consolation was that all the relationships we'd established in the church would continue.

Against the advice of Coral and other Christians I'd resigned my job in favour of a business partnership on the sales and marketing side. Contrary to everybody's expectations, the business took off. I was thrilled to be in charge of something I partly owned. The extra profit meant a better standard of living.

In summer 1981 we planned to visit Christian friends in Orlando, Florida, for three weeks. Much to our dismay, the visa forms stated that anyone convicted of manslaughter was prohibited from visiting the USA. We filled them in honestly and accurately, then prayed over them, asking God to shield the forms through the necessary channels.

Three weeks later we received our visas. God had answered our prayers. We were jubilant. Louise and Olivia were excited at the prospect of going to Disney World.

Two weeks before we were due to fly out, I arrived home from work to see Coral helping Olivia out of the car. Olivia was holding a pair of crutches.

'Guess what, Dad?'

'Don't tell me. I can't take it right now.'

It turned out that Olivia had fallen and torn her cartilage and all the ligaments affecting her knee. The hospital X-rays confirmed the worst—she'd be strapped up for six weeks. Worse still, she wouldn't be able to walk for a month.

There was only one answer. We'd have to call in the heavy mob—Ian Andrews.

Coral phoned Ian the next day. He said it was my responsibility as head of the family to ask God for Olivia's healing.

'Great—just great,' I said when I heard. 'Ian's the one with the healing gift, not me.'

'If Ian says you've got the healing word for Olivia, I believe it.'

A couple of days later, after talking to God about it, I told Olivia I was willing to pray for her if she was ready to accept God's healing now. Olivia agreed and I started to pray.

I'd barely touched her leg when she shrieked with pain.

'It hurts, Daddy, it hurts.'

'I know, but Jesus is going to heal it right now.'

I felt that God had healed her and I declared it. 'You're healed, Olivia. Now get up and walk.'

Tears still flowing, she managed to stand.

'Now take one step of faith, darling, and walk.'

'I'll try, Daddy.' She stepped forward. A broad smile came over her face as she walked across the room.

'I'm healed! I'm healed!'

Coral and I just gazed at each other. We'd seen a miracle. We took all the dressings off and there was no sign of bruising or pain.

The next day we took the dressings and crutches back to the hospital and told them of the healing Olivia had received. They couldn't believe it—even with Olivia dancing around the reception area.

From then on I never had difficulty praying for healing. Many have been healed and many haven't. But as it's God who heals and not me, I just keep on praying.

We had a tremendous holiday in the USA and returned ready to take up the next challenge.

Early in 1982 it was clear that my business was in

financial crisis. The order book was low, lease and rent on our business premises were crippling us. By May we were forced to go into voluntary liquidation.

I was devastated. Two-and-a-half years of hard work had vanished into nothing. The one area of my life I hadn't dealt with stared me in the face— failure. I was riddled with guilt as I knew I'd compromised my beliefs in some of my business dealings in the past. Now I'd lost the lot and, worse still, I owed large amounts of money.

Sid Stevens, the leader of the fellowship, was a tremendous support. He encouraged me to ask God to guide me as to where I should work and who with. Maurice Robinson was another source of encouragement. My best mate, Keith Jobber, and his wife, Betty, swung into action, taking over the legal implications of the liquidation and generally helping us while we recovered.

As the trauma died down, I realized I'd come to the end of myself. The only truth in my life that remained was Jesus Christ. Whatever happened, he was there for ever.

Coral and I chatted and prayed together. I told God I was sorry for the mess I'd got myself into and asked him to show us the way out. We waited a few weeks and then both Coral and I felt that God was telling me to start my own business.

We shared this with several close friends, who confirmed the idea. Knowing I was being guided by God gave me the confidence to do the initial spade-work.

Although we were excited about the new venture, we were desperately short of finance. All we had was £200, and our outgoings that month were £500.

One evening, after praying with and helping a young married couple, I told Coral, 'I believe God wants us to give £100 to that couple. They really need it.'

Coral was thinking the same as me: We needed the £100 as much as they did.

'If that's what God wants, then give it to them. You can't outgive God.'

I put the money in a plain envelope and at midnight put it quietly through their letterbox. Coral and I were both pleased we'd obeyed God.

We'd arranged to see the bank manager and, having prayed, arrived to see him on Monday morning.

'How can I help, Mr Fellowes?'

'I've recently seen a small company I was director of go into liquidation,' I said. 'After assessing my future, I feel God's telling me to start a new company.'

'That's an angle I haven't heard before.'

'Probably because it's the truth.'

'Why do you think the bank should lend you the money?'

'Because God wants to bless you for helping us get the new company off the ground.'

The manager looked amazed. 'How much do you need to borrow?'

'About £2000,' I half muttered.

'How much?'

'£2000.'

We discussed the new business and I produced my portfolio.

After 15 minutes of questions and answers he said, 'Well, Mr Fellowes. Thanks for being so forthright. I think we'll be able to help you.'

I looked at Coral to check if I'd heard right; she nodded.

'I don't think £2000 is a realistic figure to start your business,' he continued.

'I'll be happy with whatever you think is right.'

'I was thinking more in terms of £6000.'

I nearly fell off my chair. Unbelievable! Once my feet had touched the ground again I said, 'Thanks very much. I'm sure you won't regret it.'

'I know I won't. I'm confident you'll make it work.'

Coral and I left the bank knowing we had a £6000 overdraft facility. Everyone we told about it couldn't believe it. God had turned the bank manager round to our way of thinking.

By spring 1983 Building Crafts, my new company, was running profitably. The order book was full and many of my previous debts had been cleared. Coral and I were happy, peaceful and still head-over-heals in love with each other. It was as though we were courting again.

The final chapter of my old lifestyle had gone with my business collapse. Gone was resentment, anger, frustration, rejection, bitterness, fear of failure and, most important of all, unforgiveness. God had completely rebuilt me.

One night in July 1983 I dreamt I was watching

TV late in the evening when two men rang the door-bell.

'Mr Noel Fellowes?'

'That's me.'

I recognized the man's Lancashire accent.

The other man pushed a paper towards me and said, 'I think we've got something here that'll interest you. New revelations on a killing in 1970.'

That was it. Then I woke up. I told Coral about the dream and we both felt that God was telling me something, though we weren't sure what.

One evening in February 1984 I was working in my office at home when Coral brought in two detectives, who showed me their warrant cards.

'We've been asked to see you by the Lancashire Police about a murder investigation concerning a young man found dead in South Lancashire.'

'Why've you come to see me?'

'The victim was killed in a similar way to the one you were convicted of in 1970.'

Blood drained from my face and the adrenaline started to flow.

'For your information I was innocent of the crime in 1970. Here we are in 1984 and you're *still* trying to destroy me,' I said angrily.

Coral looked round the door and asked if everything was all right.

'No it isn't. These two are investigating a murder and they want to know about my movements. They think I've got nothing better to do than go up and down the length of England killing people.'

'They're only doing their job,' said Coral. 'I'll get the diary.'

I cooled down and apologized for my outburst. The detectives told me it was a part of their job they hated, but it had to be done if another force requested it. I gave them details of my alibi and they left.

I sat in my office for two hours completely stunned. I saw it as an attack on my whole family. Coral came in and encouraged me to keep hold of the peace I was now living in.

After she left I prayed, 'Father, I don't know that I can take any more reminders of the past. You've healed me of all the hurts and injustices. Now please put an end to it once and for all.'

I left it there, believing that the prayer would be answered in God's time.

14 The Supergrass Connection

Lenny Pilot and Fred Scott had two of the best-paid jobs in Manchester. Armed robbery wasn't just a tax-free career for them—it was a way of life.

Pilot's businesslike approach also included a mental index of all his accomplices.

Pilot and Scott had previously dabbled in more legitimate forms of commerce. Pilot had once been a smooth-talking salesman and Scott had run a string of shops dealing mainly in pornography.

The two complemented each other's criminal talents. While Scott wanted to be *au fait* with every detail, Pilot, eighteen years his junior, was known for his 'bottle'—boldly looting post offices, security trucks and company accounts departments. Both carried shotguns.

By 1982 the tie-up robbery committed by Pilot and friends on a cashier in Warsop in September 1970 was small beer. They were now in the big league.

None of their robberies took more than 90 seconds. They wore hideously wrinkled 'old-men' masks and Pilot would fire a shotgun into the ceiling if a cashier was slow at handing over the money.

Pilot would ambush security trucks, surprising the driver with both barrels of his shotgun. 'Firing shotguns was just part of the game,' he said. 'I suppose somebody would've got killed eventually.'

Greater Manchester Police Chief Jim Anderton decided to act swiftly. He ordered armed police units on 24-hour-a-day mobile duty. This later caused a furore and the plan was shelved. But Pilot and Scott laughed at the feeble attempts to trap them, enjoying a luxurious lifestyle. Soon thieving became nothing more than lucrative fun.

The post office robbery at Moston in June 1982 seemed to be just another job. Pilot parked his friend's Mercedes several miles from the crime, but a neighbour wrote down the registration number. After the gang had escaped in the Mercedes he and his associates were arrested and charge with armed robbery.

The evidence was thin and the court allowed Pilot and his gang bail while the case was prepared.

During the 12 months before the trial, five similar attacks took place. Detective Sergeant Henri Exton tried to persuade Pilot to turn informer, but Pilot was having nothing to do with it.

Scott had other ideas. He felt that the police had a strong case against him on the Moston robbery. (He was right, and the pair were jailed for 10 years.) So he decided to turn 'supergrass'—informing on his partners in crime.

Under a false name, he travelled from Walton prison—where I'd served the first few months of my sentence—to Wigan police station. There he started 'singing like a canary'. He admitted armed raids topping £100,000 in cash. He was later jailed for seven years for these crimes—but the judge ordered them to be concurrent so they wouldn't lengthen his 10-year sentence.

While Scott was still supposed to be at Walton, Pilot was starting his sentence at Strangeways. Henri Exton presented Pilot with a mass of evidence gained from Scott and then offered Pilot supergrass status. He declined.

Operation Belgium in the New Year of 1984 involved 200 officers in dawn swoops on thirty homes, all acting on information from Scott.

At that point Pilot knew he had to act fast. He claims he turned his back on his former profession. 'I had enough of crimes and criminals and decided I'd co-operate fully and not only corroborate Scott but help police clear up other serious crimes.'

Pilot was moved to Lancaster Castle—scene of my trial—until his supergrass status was confirmed. His name was changed temporarily to Robert Downes and he was released into the hands of police guardians.

Pilot's uncanny knack of remembering names and places produced a flood of details on crimes. In return, he was apparently given considerable freedom.

Pilot's information gave rise to *Operation Holland* and the arrest of around twenty men. Two stood out from the rest—Billy Clark and Joey Berry.

On 13 February, 1984 Pilot owned up to the Moston robbery and confirmed twenty-one previous convictions, including the Morecambe optician assault and theft in 1972.

Then he began talking about the Overton crime.

In 1970 Joey Berry had come to see Pilot. 'He said he and our mate Billy Clark had been to do a tie-up and Billy had hit this bloke and the bloke had died. Joe was frightened he could get done for murder.

'He said a businessman dealing in one-armed bandits had told him and Billy about a retired coin-dealer who lived Morecambe way, had a safe with plenty of money in it and some valuable coins, and it'd be an easy tie-up. Joe said the bloke had let them in. Billy had given him a crack and the bloke had died.

'Some time later I was in Risley remand centre. There was a lot of talk among the staff and cons about an ex-cop who'd been done for a murder in Morecambe of a coin-dealer. I remember one of the staff telling me that the ex-cop was a nuisance, always going on about his innocence. At the time I thought, "The man's innocent. There can't possibly be two murders of coin-dealers in Morecambe." '

Pilot recalled one more detail. 'I remember Joey saying on that night something about the tide having to be out so they could get to the house.'

The first job for the police was to find records and files to confirm a killing had taken place in the Morecambe area. Excitement grew as the name Harold Parkinson came up.

The police operation was led by Detective Chief Superintendent Bill Lumsden, his last major case before retiring. He handed the Clark assignment to Detective Chief Inspector Allan Potts. On 13 March, doors were kicked in and Clark and Berry were arrested.

After persistent questioning, Clark admitted to involvement in the Warsop tie-up robbery but refused to budge on the Overton killing.

Potts pointed out the similarities between the two jobs. 'The man at Warsop was tied up with Sellotape and bandages while the man at Morecambe was tied up with webbing and electric cord, all wrapped in similar positions on the body of each man.'

Clark realized he was walking on quicksand and made no reply.

Potts asked, 'Does the name Fellowes mean anything to you?'

'Never heard of him.'

'We believe the two of you got into the Overton home using a collector's coin. That, once in, you both tied him up.'

Clark held his head for several minutes, then came six simple words: 'I did it on my own.'

Clark then recalled how he'd gone to Parkinson's house and shown him some coins. 'He went upstairs and I was rooting around to see what I could find. I got £55 and shoved it in my pocket.'

He described how the old man had caught him in the act. 'He jumped on my back and started hitting me with karate chops. We were fighting for a while, then he just went on the floor and was gasping for breath.

'I had to tie him up so he couldn't follow me. Then I ran out of the front door and went back to the pub. We got a taxi to the station and a train back to Manchester.'

Clark had hit him only with his fists. 'I didn't mean to hurt him. I just wanted to get away.'

His recall of 14 years ago was crystal clear. Back in Manchester he'd worried about the old man left tied in the lonely cottage. It was he who phoned Lancashire police and reported an accident at 19 Main Street.

'How come you remember the address?'

'I've lived with it for 14 years.'

He wasn't the only one!

Later, Clarke added, 'I've been told that a man called Fellowes was convicted of this job, but he didn't have any part in it. I'm very sorry it happened this way.'

Meanwhile, after much persistence, police got Joey Berry to make a statement. He'd travelled to Overton with the others and stayed in the pub while Clarke disappeared to commit the crime. He'd originally planned to join in a 'sneak thief' of the coin collection but his courage had deserted him.

Years later he'd heard about 'a kid getting time for murder' in Morecambe but had never heard of the name Fellowes.

Three teams of officers travelled to Overton.

'Around 800 statements were taken at the time of

the incident, many of them since destroyed,' recalls Potts. 'But we recovered more than thirty from Lancaster station. We were less successful trying to trace fingerprints taken at the house because they'd long since been destroyed by the criminal records office.'

The *Lancashire Evening Post* gave the story front-page treatment. But missing was the location of the man who'd been convicted in the first place. Crime reporter Bob Westerdale found a former neighbour who remembered I'd originally come from the Windsor area. After sweet-talking the phone operator, Westerdale got my address despite my ex-directory status. Before long, he and Terry Bromley, a photographer, set off down the motorway.

I was watching soccer on TV one night when the doorbell rang. Slightly annoyed that I might miss a vital goal, I rushed to answer the door.

'Yes, what is it?'

Standing on the doorstep were two strangers.

'Noel Fellowes?'

'Yes, that's me.'

'I've got some very important news about the Overton killing.'

He produced a newspaper and offered it to me.

'Two men are being questioned about it.'

They didn't know that those few words were a rerun of the dream I'd had in 1983.

'I've waited 14 years for this. Come in. You're messengers from God.'

They looked puzzled.

'Don't worry. I'll explain later.'

I shouted to Coral upstairs. 'Come down. I've got some really exciting news.'

She was down in a flash.

'Let me introduce you to Bob Westerdale and Terry Bromley from the *Lancashire Evening Post*. They're here to break the news about new developments in the Overton killing.'

Coral and I hugged each other and read the story over and over again. I was shaking with excitement.

'At last. It's finally going to be sorted out.'

Bob and Terry just sat there while I kept leaping up and down praising God for answered prayer.

When I'd calmed down Bob pressed me for a response so he could run a headline story the next day. Coral and I decided to call Sid Stevens for a third opinion. He and his wife Ann came round in minutes.

Bob felt he'd lost the moment. 'Why can't you decide yourself?'

'We need wisdom. Besides, the press haven't got the best record in the honesty stakes. I need to protect Coral and the children and make sure that I have witnesses to verify what I actually say.'

We talked over the issues and decided that I should give Bob a story. I set out the rules for the interview to protect my family, and I offered Bob exclusive rights. When I related my dream in 1983, Bob sat there open-mouthed.

'I told you I thought you were God's messengers and I firmly believe he's selected you to report everything I have to say.'

'I give you my word I won't let you down.'

Bob was relaxed, blunt and a fellow Manchester United supporter, which was even better. It was 2.30 in the morning when we'd finished. Bob and Terry were delighted with the quality of the material and left to write their story, which had to be phoned through by breakfast-time to catch the early issues of the paper.

Coral and I talked with Sid and Ann until about 3.30. We were both too excited to sleep.

These were early days, but we thanked God for making the all-important breakthrough on my behalf.

15 'I Am Innocent!'

'I am innocent.' Those three words were the headline on the front page of the *Lancashire Evening Post*. My trust in Bob had been repaid. It was the start of a firm friendship.

I was quoted as saying, 'I am absolutely innocent. Now I want my name cleared.' That summed it up. Now was the time for everyone to know I wasn't a killer.

Within a few days I travelled to Salford with Ian Andrews to meet Detective Chief Superintendent Lumsden, who was spearheading the Overton enquiry. I wanted Ian with me because of my last encounter with police officers in 1970. Also I valued Ian's discernment of people.

As it turned out, Bill Lumsden was a delightful man. Ian and I were satisfied that my side of things was safe in his hands. Lumsden advised me to get a good lawyer.

I already had one—Graham Hughes, of Robinson, Jarvis & Rolf on the Isle of Wight. Ian had advised me that his friend, Clive Rolf, a Christian lawyer, was the man to contact. He in turn passed me to his partner, Graham, who specialized in criminal law.

After our meeting Bill Lumsden told the press, 'He has no animosity towards the police and wished us every success in our enquiry. I have a very open mind on his guilt or innocence and we're working hard to establish the truth.'

Off the record he told Bob, 'You'll do well to stick with this story; it's going to get more and more interesting.'

Coral and I travelled to the Isle of Wight to meet Graham Hughes.

'How do you feel about handling the case totally on my behalf?' I asked.

'It'll be my privilege, Noel. I'll endeavour to make sure nothing goes wrong this time.'

Graham paid attention to detail. I had complete trust in him. Before we left his office, we prayed, asking God to help Graham every step of the way.

Coral and I returned home secure in the knowledge that both Bob Westerdale and Graham Hughes were fighting all the way for us.

The first information Detective Chief Superintendent Lumsden latched on to was the reported three sightings of Harold Parkinson on Wednesday February 25, 1970—the day after the Crown claimed I killed him.

Retired fisherman Jimmy Braid, who'd described talking to Parkinson over the back garden, stuck by his earlier statement. But barman Charles Ramsey, who'd told Mounsey's officers he had 'easily recognized him', now had other ideas: 'Even now I'm not positively sure it was Parkinson... I'd had a few drinks.'

Bus driver Richard Luke was more positive. He'd said fourteen years earlier that Parkinson had 'lifted his hand to me in acknowledgement when he saw me'. What he hadn't said at the time was that he'd stopped and given Parkinson a ride to Heysham village. In admitting that in 1970, he could have been in trouble because his official trip wasn't scheduled to start for another half an hour.

Meanwhile, Lenny Pilot faced a judge forty miles away at Preston Crown Court. Every national newspaper was represented. They were intrigued by Pilot's supergrass activities and the spin-off statement he'd made concerning Overton. Pilot pleaded guilty to twenty-three charges. Several times he peered nervously at the locked doorway to the court as if expecting retribution from the Manchester gang-land he'd turned his back on.

In all, Pilot had netted £121,000 in his various raids, and a further £42,000 in thirty other offences he asked the court to take into consideration.

Detective Superintendent Bernard McGourlay complimented Pilot on the quality of his information, which had resulted in a confession rate of 70 per cent.

The barrister drew attention to the Overton killing and to Clark. 'If any question arises of a man having been wrongly convicted in the past, Pilot's information may well serve to right that wrong.'

Jailing Pilot for six and a half years—concurrent with the ten he was already serving—Mr Justice McNeill remarked: 'You career in crime is finished. No criminal will ever trust you again.'

Five days later, Lancashire Chief Constable Brian Johnson decided to send Lumsden's report on the Overton crime to the Director of Public Prosecutions.

Bob Westerdale had pledged to protect Coral and the children by not printing my address. But he warned that it was only a matter of time before a rival got hold of it.

In late May, seven weeks after the *Evening Post* had traced me, I was confronted by a *Daily Mail* reporter and photographer. I showed them quotes used by the *Evening Post* and they agreed not to take my picture.

Some hours later, I spotted a camera lens zooming on me from a car parked down the road. I knew I'd been betrayed. With a screech of tyres, the car disappeared. A phone call to the paper's London office had little effect. The story was used two days later with an unflattering picture of me and quotes I scarcely recognized.

The encounter didn't spoil my relationship with Bob, who booked us in at a hotel in Morecambe. His idea was to upstage the *Mail* by taking legitimate photos and writing a cover story.

The next morning we travelled to Overton, the first time for me since 1970. Terry Bromley took pictures of me outside Parkinson's house. Then I noticed an elderly man enter the house.

'Excuse me, is this your house?' I asked.

'It sure is. You from the press?'

'No. My name's Noel Fellowes. I'm the man convicted of killing Parkinson in 1970 and I'm fighting to have my name cleared.'

'So you're the unfortunate man who suffered all those years? My name's Ernest Staples. Would you like to come in?'

I could hardly contain myself.

'It'd be nice to see the room where I was supposed to have killed the poor man.'

'Hang on and I'll ask the wife if it's OK.'

A few seconds later he waved me in through his front door and invited Bob and me into the sitting room. A chill ran up my spine. I recalled the photos Mounsey kept thrusting in my face in 1970. Now I was standing in the room where it actually happened.

'So this is where it all took place?'

'Yes, I'm afraid so.'

'I wish it was all finished and they could leave the poor man to rest in peace,' said Mr Staples tearfully.

'Do you still feel a presence in your house, Mrs Staples?' I enquired.

'Yes. I wish he'd rest.'

'You've probably read in the papers that I'm now a Christian. I'd like to pray over everything that happened in this room all those years ago.'

'We'd be grateful if you would.'

I asked God to bring his peace back into the house and to rid the place of unwanted spirits. I prayed over every room and, within minutes, peace had returned to the house and its occupants.

Mr and Mrs Staples thanked me and said they felt much better.

'It's been my privilege to meet you and share these moments with you.'

I felt really honoured. Turning to Bob I said, 'It's incredible. God's brought me 250 miles to visit the house and indeed the room where the crime was committed. On top of that, he's commissioned me to pray over all that took place here.'

'Nothing surprises me any more where you're concerned, Noel. It's just amazing.'

That evening the newspaper headline read 'Convicted ex-PC prays at house of death'.

The *Daily Mail* had truly been upstaged.

A month later a full-scale enquiry was launched and Eric Evans, North Wales Deputy Chief Constable, was chosen to head it.

He had at his disposal two Detective Chief Inspectors—Allan Potts, who'd already proved himself in Overton, and Tom Eyres. They set up an incident room at Morecambe police station. A dozen men began sifting through mountains of details and interviewing 300 people from as far apart as Sussex and Cumbria.

Eric Evans recalls: 'We couldn't find a transcript of the trial in 1970 and most of the police papers had been disposed of. The time gap was insurmountable for some witnesses; we were unable to get much detailed information for instance from either Mr Mounsey or Mr Sanderson Temple. But that, of course, is understandable.'

The squad started with the first man to discover the body—Bernard Darby. 'I noticed that he was tied up with various articles including a purple scarf and paisley patterned cravat,' he told them. 'I believe both articles were his own property.'

The cleaning lady, Mrs Josephine Hockenhull, took a similar line. 'His favourite items were with-out doubt his cravats. The cloth covering his chin [shown to her in a police photo] is a purplish-coloured loose-cover from off the back of the couch.'

How could this crucial evidence about the purple cloth have been overlooked all those years ago? At my trial Mrs Hockenhull hadn't been asked about any of the bindings or clothing.

Eric Evans decided to approach two other witnesses—my ex-wife and my former mother-in-law.

Michele told him, 'The police believed I or my family may have hired a private detective to get evidence for my divorce. I told them that was utter nonsense. I didn't need any further evidence as my lawyer already had ample grounds. I've always felt strongly that he'd been wrongly convicted.

'The other thing that puzzled me about the trial was that the property missing from the house was never mentioned. It was never suggested that robbery might have been the motive.'

Her mother, Mrs Iris Castagnini, explained that coal deliveries had come monthly and that her husband always dealt with the bills. In late February 1970 two detectives showed her a picture of Parkinson and asked why her name and address appeared in a book at his house.

'When they told me it was a coal receipt that had been paid to a man who represented the coal firm, I realized he was the person my husband paid when he called at the house.

'I then spoke to them about Noel being in the police some time ago and that he was a "villain"—something of a jack-the-lad. I didn't mean this in any malicious way.'

The team checked the quality of the evidence from the nightclub pair, John Bamborough and Carey Thornton. The former had changed his name to Omega and was traced to Keighley, Yorkshire. He was asked about my joking remarks. 'I thought it was all bravado. I can't remember if I said that in court.'

It took longer to find Thornton, who was now a computer salesman in Leeds. 'I was what you'd call prompted,' he admitted. 'I'd never heard the name Parkinson before. I can recall being shown a plastic bag with what appeared to be a purple scarf. It was never taken out and shown to me properly. I was led to believe that my evidence was being used to assist Noel Fellowes. It came as a big shock to me when Noel was convicted.'

Some information came their way without any effort. Parkinson's next-door neighbour, Ronald Carey, had given Mounsey's men a blurred description of two men standing on Main Street. Now he talked of two men in their twenties coming out of Parkinson's house. 'One of them shouted, "We'll see you then, Harold," after looking in my direction and seeming hesitant.'

One former Chief Superintendent, Alf Collins, revealed how much John Bamborough had it in for me. 'I was on duty at Lancaster police station when I received a phone call at 3.00a.m. from John Bamborough. He said we'd got the right man for the Parkinson murder.'

Not everyone co-operated. Former police constable Alan Knowles had taken the phone message about an accident on Main Street. 'I'm out of the police now,' he said curtly. 'If you want me to give evidence you'll have to subpoena me.'

My lawyer, Graham Hughes, confirmed that Eric Evans wanted to interview me. He travelled from Wales to Reading, where Graham and I met him on 23 August, 1984.

Evans was a tall, middle-aged man with silver-grey hair and a gentle yet authoritative voice. He was a wise old fox beneath the warm smile and relaxed manner.

His only objective, he told us, was to establish the truth. Who it affected wasn't his problem. There were three options: that there were no grounds to doubt my conviction; that there were insufficient grounds to suggest that any further action should be taken; or that the enquiry cast great doubt on my conviction and I should be allowed to continue my appeal against it.

He considered the third option to be the one he'd most likely recommend, though he couldn't, of course, speak for the Director of Public Prosecutions.

I was thrilled. At last things seemed to be moving favourably in my direction.

As the last person to be interviewed in his enquiry, I was asked numerous questions about the events in 1970. I answered them honestly and openly. Unlike the last interview I'd had with a senior police officer in 1970, this one was both pleasant and fulfilling.

We spent a long time establishing the fact that I was convicted of killing Parkinson on the Tuesday night or early Wednesday morning. Evans was now almost certain that Parkinson met his death on the Wednesday evening.

One of the greatest surprises was when Evans produced copies of taxi record sheets covering the time of the killing. I'd carried the can for the fact that they were missing. These sheets may have been lying among documents actually in court during my trial. If only they'd been produced at the trial, things could have worked out so differently.

At the end of the interview I asked, 'Do you believe I had nothing at all to do with Parkinson's killing? It's important to know, and I'll understand if you want to answer off the record.'

Eric Evans looked me straight in the eye. 'Absolutely not. I believe you're innocent.'

'I appreciate your honesty and pray that everything you need to establish the truth will be forthcoming.'

'It's been a pleasure to meet you, Mr Fellowes.'

On Thursday August 2, officers Evans and Potts charged Billy Clark with the manslaughter of

Harold Parkinson. The following day he appeared at the magistrates' court in Manchester and was remanded in custody at Strangeways prison for a week.

On August 16 the Director of Public Prosecutions ruled that Joey Berry, the other man linked with the Overton crime, would not face any charges.

Berry later told Bob Westerdale how he and the others had hoped to find £25,000 worth of gold coins in Parkinson's house. He also spoke of his hatred for Lenny Pilot, who'd betrayed him.

In October, Pilot was released from prison into the custody of armed Manchester police, in readiness for the *Operation Holland* and *Belgium* trials, to be held at Lancaster Castle. At the end of the trials, he disappeared to a prison with a supergrass unit.

Meanwhile, Eric Evans had completed his enquiries in the Morecambe area and sent his squad of officers back to their separate bases. He was pleased that at the end of his mission there was no mudslinging at the discredited forensic scientist Dr Alan Clift who, in Evans' eyes, had been unfairly pilloried.

'The case against Noel Fellowes wasn't strong to begin with and our enquiries make it a lot weaker still,' he said in an interview with Bob Westerdale. 'This has been a unique job... complicated—but always interesting.

'But my satisfaction will have been to assist an innocent man to prove his innocence.'

16 Truth On Trial

After all my frustrating years of waiting for a major development, the months preceding Billy Clark's trial were among the worst. It was finally scheduled for Wednesday 17 April, 13 months after his arrest.

Much of the delay was because of demands from the star witness, Lenny Pilot, including the need for special police protection because of his supergrass activities. In one letter Pilot described how he could hardly eat or sleep as the trial date neared and he eventually collapsed on the eve of it.

I'd considered attending part of the hearing. But I didn't want to distract the jury members who might be comparing Clark with me as we sat in different parts of the same courtroom.

The judge was Sir Joseph Cantley, OBE, whose attention to detail and concentrated thoroughness were legendary.

The stage was similar and the script closely followed the opening lines of my trial fifteen years before. The only difference was that the lead performance was being played by Billy Clark, not Noel Fellowes.

Mrs Helen Grindrod QC opened the case concerning Parkinson's death, saying, 'The prosecution say that he died on the evening of the 25th and whoever tied him up was responsible for his death.'

She then uttered the words I'd been longing to hear for a third of my life: 'On 8 March, 1970 a man named Keith Noel Fellowes was arrested for the murder of Harold Parkinson. He was tried and convicted of manslaughter on 29 June, 1970. The Crown now say that was a tragic mistake.'

The reporters couldn't write it down fast enough. Bob Westerdale phoned me with the news. I was overjoyed by the content of the Crown's admission at such an early stage.

Mrs Grindrod described how Clark entered the house, rooted through the old man's belongings and assaulted him before tying him up. She also introduced the importance of two phone calls by Clark—one to the victim and the other to Lancaster police.

The first witness was former Lancashire policeman Alan Knowles, who'd refused to help officers the previous year. He said he'd received a phone call saying there'd been an accident in Main Street. Next, police constable Joseph Howarth told how he was called out to Overton to investigate the phone message. Both men confirmed that they hadn't given this information at my court hearing in 1970.

A statement by Bernard Darby, the man who discovered Parkinson's body, was read out. Then

Mrs Josephine Hockenhull took the stand. Slides of the victim were projected on to a screen and Mrs Hockenhull pointed out a number of the bindings on the body she could identify.

Eric Evans was waiting for her to mention the all-important purple material, masking the lower half of the battered victim's face. This was the cloth that was supposed to have been my cravat but which Mrs Hockenhull identified as coming from Parkinson's couch. Somehow the evidence slipped her mind and she left the witness-box.

The situation wasn't irreversible. The following day Mrs Hockenhull made a surprise reappearance to tell the judge about the purple cloth. She seemed to enjoy her fleeting time in the limelight.

The harrowing photos of the body stayed on the screen most of the morning as the man who took them, retired Detective Sergeant George Brogden, explained the nature of the bonds. He said it had later taken several hours to remove them in the morgue. He, too, hadn't been near the court for my hearing.

Joey Berry, the petty villain who'd been told he wouldn't be charged over the Overton crime, described in slang that needed translating how he'd lost his courage about robbing the coin collector and stayed in the pub with cockney Pete while Berry disappeared.

Detective Chief Inspector Potts read out the interview he had with Clark: 'I did it on my own. I got £55 and shoved it in my pocket. He jumped on my back and started hitting me with karate chops. I had to tie him up so he couldn't follow me.'

Clark lowered his face as each sentence seemed more incriminating than the last. 'I never meant to harm him. I suppose I'll get twenty years for this.'

Mr Michael Maguire's cross-examination of Potts tried to raise a doubt against the case that had gone against his client so badly thus far.

'In 1970 were all the exhibits considered relevant put before the jury?'

'Probably, yes.'

'Fellowes was a taxi driver. Was there some connection between Fellowes and the deceased?'

'In the deceased's house there was a notebook with Fellowes' mother-in-law's address. He was a debt-collector.'

'It was also believed in the village that Mr Parkinson was not only a debt-collector but a private investigator. Was that fact known to Fellowes?'

'I think it probably was.'

'The enquiry was conducted by senior police officers under Joe Mounsey. The case was put before magistrates. There were committal proceedings and Noel Fellowes was charged with murder. A jury convicted him of manslaughter. Was the 1984 enquiry deprived of seeing most of those exhibits?'

'Yes.'

Maguire added that no fingerprint evidence was now available. He was suddenly gaining the upper hand—and Billy Clark was about to give evidence on his own behalf.

The court was full for the dramatic event. It came as a surprise when Clark said early on that, 'apart from a few slight differences', he agreed with Potts' account of the interview after his arrest.

Clark thought originally that Parkinson had been manually strangled. He admitted he'd tied up the old man. But he claimed, 'Things were done to him that were completely wrong to what I'd done to him. I compared how I tied him up and how the papers said he'd been tied up.'

He said he didn't apply webbing, the purple material gagging his mouth and white bandage across his chest. He'd left him near the centre of the room. 'His legs were straight and he was all right. Just a bit out of breath.'

Clark surmised that cockney Pete could have got into the cottage to steal the coins and finish him off. Or it could have been me. 'I'd clear Mr Fellowes if I could. I'd say I did it. But there are too many things wrong.'

Clark said he couldn't understand why the man had died. 'I thought I was responsible for him dying because I wasn't aware of the full facts. It's time to tell the truth. Joe Berry had nothing to do with it. As far as I knew then, Noel Fellowes had nothing to do with it. If I could clear him, I would do. If I'd done these things, I'd plead guilty to them.'

At this point Clark became agitated, even telling the judge I was an 'out-and-out murderer'. He composed himself under cross-examination.

'I stopped thinking I was responsible when I saw in the paper that Noel Fellowes was being remanded every week. After so long there'd been nothing in the paper and I took it for granted that Noel Fellowes had been released with no charges whatsoever.

'I blamed myself all the time. I thought for fourteen years it was the flex that killed the man. The feelings of guilt weren't lifted until I read the pathologist's report.'

All the newspapers were represented in court. The *Daily Mail* used a story headed 'Clear me, pleads jailed PC', quoting me in full. They must have spoken to another Noel Fellowes. I'd vowed not to help them after they let me down the first time.

The prosecution and defence lawyers gave their summaries on Friday and the judge adjourned the hearing until Monday morning.

The suspense of waiting was becoming over-powering for me and I took up Bob Westerdale's offer to bring my family up to stay at his home until after the verdict.

I agreed to do one radio interview in Lancashire, embargoed until after the Clark case was over. They wanted two alternative reactions from me—one to Clark's conviction and another to his acquittal. That seemed strange—I hadn't thought about Clark walking free after the balance of evidence.

We relaxed most of the weekend and I was left to pace Bob's house alone on Monday.

Meanwhile, Mr Justice Cantley was summing up:

'We don't know what evidence there was against Mr Fellowes but there must have been some which pointed to him as the guilty man, or he wouldn't have been convicted. On the other hand, it'd seem that there was absent from that trial any information at all pointing to, or even mentioning, this defendant.

'The prosecution say that conviction was a tragic mistake and Mr Fellowes was innocent of the charge. If that's right, and this defendant before you is the real guilty man, it certainly was a tragic mistake and it's disturbing to any lawyer to think it could happen.'

After mulling over the main points of the case, judge and jury retired and Clark was taken away to suffer the same nail-biting tension I'd undergone all those years earlier.

Two hours later, the jury filed back into court. Clark sat on the edge of his seat, his eyes fixed on the foreman.

'Not guilty.'

Applause and cheering erupted in the public gallery and a wide grin broke from Clark's face. Some of the police officers tried to hide their disappointment.

But the court hadn't finished with Clark yet. He pleaded guilty to robbing Warsop Town Hall clerk Neal Hunt of £660, the crime committed with Lenny Pilot back in September 1970. The full list of his previous convictions was read out, starting 20 years earlier.

The judge told him: 'You're a persistent criminal and unjustifiably pleased with yourself. Tying somebody up is a serious aggravated burglary.'

Taking into account his pleas of guilty, he sent Clark to jail for four years.

Bob's phone call to me was full of awkward silences. I was shell-shocked, and back to square one. In a deep depression, I realized that everybody would still think I'd done it. How could I ever pick myself up?

Coral was doing her best to find a thread of reason in the whole catastrophe. She kept repeating that she knew God was in charge.

At 6.00p.m., after dinner, the others left me alone in the kitchen. My ears pricked up as I heard the Clark case being discussed on TV. The final few words confirmed Coral's pledge: 'Tonight the Home Office said they would consider as a matter of urgency the plea by former policeman Noel Fellowes for a declaration of innocence.'

Yippee! The Clark verdict would have no bearing on my quest for vindication. Suddenly, the atmosphere was transformed. It was party time—we were going to an expensive restaurant with Bob and his family!

It was remarkable how our depression had been banished by those few words. God was on the move.

The following day I did a TV interview. A question-and-answer session was transmitted into millions of homes in the north-west three times during the day. I returned home bursting with enthusiasm for the next event in this dramatic story.

Within days, Home Secretary Leon Brittan sliced through red tape to secure me an early listing in the Appeal Court.

I knew my goal was almost achieved. And this time I wouldn't be denied.

17 Free Indeed!

Even before the Home Secretary referred my case back to the Court of Appeal, my lawyer Graham Hughes had engaged a top London barrister—Ian Hughes—to fight my case. (It was sheer coincidence that both men shared the same name.)

After looking at the documents from 1970 and 1984, Ian Hughes wrote a 17-page document that favoured every aspect of my grounds for appeal. I had the best legal counsel—I was sure this was all God's work—and I could now sort out other areas of my life.

After the Clark trial I felt cheated and resentful with the result. But I'd been convicted for a crime I never committed, so who was I to judge another man on the basis of new evidence, whether he actually meant to kill or not? In my heart I still felt that justice hadn't been done on my behalf.

After praying about it with Coral I realized that God's way wasn't necessarily my way. I'd been so mentally, emotionally and physically involved in the case that I'd stopped listening to what God was saying. It had become *my* battle, *my* injustice, *my* case.

Also, my whole life as a Christian had been thrown into turmoil. Following a number of unresolved problems, Coral and I had decided to leave our Christian fellowship. It seemed like the end, but God had a future for us. I recognized that he was teaching me something for the future.

We were invited to attend a guest service at Bracknell Baptist Church by our friends, Keith and Betty Jobber. We hadn't been to the church since we left years before, but we decided to go. Everyone responded warmly to us. We felt we'd come back home, and that God wanted us to return to the church where we'd first known him.

We continued to attend the church services, but I was nervous about committing myself to the church before the appeal had been heard. Coral had filled in her commitment form to join the church. She asked why I hadn't filled in mine.

'I'm sure that's where we're meant to be, but I'd rather wait till the appeal's finished. Then I'll be able to decide. If it all goes against me, I really don't know how I'll react.'

'That's all right, love. Let's wait until you're sure.'

Two weeks before the appeal, I woke up one morning and sat on the edge of the bed. Suddenly I had an incredible revelation of Calvary—I pictured Jesus on the cross, suffering such a painful, undignified, cruel death. He hadn't deserved it, yet he'd died for me.

I sat there shaking my head. 'Oh, Lord. Forgive me for my attitude.'

Something broke inside me as I realized that Jesus Christ had given his life for me.

I fell on my knees. 'God, whatever happens in the Appeal Court, I'm still going on with you. You're the only truth. I want to fulfil everything you've planned for in my life.'

I stayed there, drinking it all in, when a soft voice whispered in my head. 'I know your heart, Noel. I know your heartbeat's for me.'

'It sure is, God.'

Excitedly, I hurried to the dining-room and told Coral. 'God's given me an amazing revelation of Calvary. He's broken through the defences I was building around the appeal.'

Coral was delighted. We hugged, and I told her everything that had happened in the bedroom.

'That's wonderful. Isn't God good?' she said, tears streaming down her face.

We thanked God for his timely word and filled in the commitment forms. We were home, both with God and the church. What more could we ask?

We were now rapidly approaching the appeal date. We were going to be heard in the top court in the land before the Lord Chief Justice of England, Lord Lane. Since my revelation from God I'd enjoyed a new peace and a deeper assurance about my vindication.

I'd arranged for Bob Westerdale to stay with us and for Keith Jobber to drive us to the Appeal Court in London.

Bob arrived in the late afternoon of 11 July. After dinner, things really started to hot up. Friends and relations kept popping in to see us and wish us well for the appeal hearing.

It was well after midnight before we went to bed. I woke to the sound of the alarm clock. It was 6.15a.m. on 12 July, 1985. The big day had arrived. I was nervous and had a feeling of nausea. In a few hours' time I knew that the final chapter would be written and I'd be either ecstatic or devastated.

'Keep walking in faith. Keep feeding on God's promises,' I said to myself.

Keith arrived at 7.15. Coral, Bob and I jumped in the car and we headed for London. Most of the journey was spent in relative silence, locked in our own individual thoughts.

We arrived outside the law courts at 8.10, parked and consulted the listings, to see which court we were in.

As I walked through the courts hand in hand with Coral, I felt a sense of walking through the corridors of legal history. How many people had come here over the centuries hoping to find the justice that had escaped them for so long? If only walls could speak.

We went to a cafe and had a breakfast of bacon sandwiches and coffee. I could feel the tension mounting. Nine o'clock. Another hour and we'd be in court.

I'd arranged to meet Graham Hughes inside the court building between 9.15 and 9.30. He looked in the same state as us—excited and nervous. He said he'd got up three times in the night to pray.

'You're in safe company,' I said. 'Coral, Keith and I have been praying since we woke up this morning.'

Graham wanted to show me the brief for the proceedings but I declined. I wanted to stand in the faith God had given me—not muddle myself with a lot of information.

The place was a hive of activity. The four of us stood in a small circle and prayed for Graham and Ian Hughes and for the three judges.

At 9.55 we walked into the court. I sat with Coral and Keith, just behind my counsel. The press-box was full; Bob acknowledged me with a wave and a smile.

As the court clerk asked everyone to rise for the entrance of the judges, a shock-wave shot through my body. It reminded me of my trial fifteen years earlier. I was before the High Court once again. And my whole life rested in their hands, or so it seemed.

I was sweating and my limbs shook.

Suddenly Jesus' words came to memory: 'Where two or three are gathered together in my name, I am there in the midst of them.' There was Coral, Keith, Graham, myself—and Jesus. 'Welcome to the proceedings, Jesus. Please take over.'

Ian Hughes opened the case. 'Mr Fellowes' conviction for manslaughter on 29 June, 1970 is unsafe and unsatisfactory for the reasons I intend to bring before the court this morning.'

He outlined the relevant points. The purple cravat supposedly belonging to me had been identified as belonging to the deceased. Dr Alan Clift, the forensic biologist, had found no clear evidence to link me with the death of the deceased. I'd faced a twelve-hour ordeal of interviews in an effort to obtain an admission of guilt.

My nervousness was gone and I was growing in confidence with every word spoken.

Ian Hughes referred to the missing taxi records, which hadn't been missing at all. He went on to my apparent motive—that I was being followed by the deceased. It was now known, indeed had always been known, that my mother-in-law's name was in the deceased man's notebook not as a private investigation but as a coal debt.

Parkinson had met his death not on the Tuesday night or early Wednesday morning, but on Wednesday night, for which I'd always had a cast-iron alibi. He concluded that, had Clark's evidence been available in 1970, I would never have been charged.

As Ian Hughes sat down, I felt like giving him a round of thunderous applause for his efforts.

I whispered in Keith's ear. 'How do you think it's going?'

'No problem. We're on a winner all the way.'

Lord Lane then invited Mr Clegg, counsel for the Crown, to present his case. He said he felt his colleague, Mr Hughes, had covered the case thoroughly. The Crown had nothing to add except to say it was a disturbing case all round.

I could hardly believe my ears. The Crown weren't raising any objections to my appeal! There was a definite buzz in the courtroom. Everyone, it seemed, had been taken by surprise.

A new nervousness gripped me, one of excitement. It took all my inner discipline to refrain from jumping up and thanking Mr Clegg personally for making such a decision.

The three judges huddled together before Lord Lane pronounced his verdict.

'It would be an understatement to say that this is an extremely disturbing case,' he said. 'If it does nothing else, it demonstrates the fallibility of any system which is operated by human beings. One hopes that many of the disquieting features which emerged from this case would no longer take place.'

What a staggering opening from the Lord Chief Justice of England! Lord Lane outlined the background to the case, including the finding of my mother-in-law's name in Parkinson's book and the alleged opportunity I'd had as a taxi-driver to get from my place of work to kill the victim.

'The third matter was that he'd allegedly made admissions to acquaintances and to the police, or, if not admissions, references to the killing which might on one view be construed as admission of guilt. Fourthly, it was alleged that he told lies to the police.'

Fifteen years later and Lord Lane was saying I allegedly told lies to the police. All I'd ever done was make flippant remarks which could have been in bad taste. I'd told the police the *truth*; it was *they* who'd refused to accept it. Surely he wasn't going to do a whitewash job where the police were concerned?

He continued: 'It has now been proved conclusively to the satisfaction of this court that this man did not commit this crime. As with the case of all disasters, whether they be forensic disasters or any other kind of disaster, it was a combination of events which led to this miscarriage of justice; a combination of misfortunes, one must also say misbehaviours or errors, and of mistaken conclusions which conspired to produce the result.'

It was over. I was going to be vindicated. 'You've won, Noel,' I thought. 'It's over; you're free.'

At the same time Coral was hugging me, fighting back tears of joy because it was over for her as well, all the heartache and suffering she'd endured, coping with me over the years. Ian and Graham Hughes both turned towards me in congratulation and Bob gave a victory smile and salute from the press-box.

After further background information, Lord Lane concluded: 'Accordingly, this appeal, for that is how the reference from the Home Secretary dated 7 May, 1985 must be treated, is allowed and the con-viction is quashed.'

Coral and I sat there, lost in our own thoughts. It was over and I was totally and universally vindicated. Graham Hughes applied for costs backdated to April 1984 when I'd engaged him. They were granted.

Tears formed in my eyes, tears of relief and joy. I brushed them off, continuing to sit in my moment of triumph. 'Thank you, Father,' I kept saying to God.

For years I'd wondered how I'd feel when the whole nightmare was over. Now I felt as though a heavy weight had been removed from my life. A mental video gave me instant playback of the last fifteen years. The good times, the bad times, the in-between times.

'What a privilege!'

'Pardon?' said Coral.

'What a privilege to have been used like this.'

It seemed stupid, but I really meant it. We descended from the court into a small passageway and handed out congratulations to each other. Everyone was overjoyed. Justice had been done.

The press were waiting, eager to interview Coral and me.

Ian Hughes said, 'You're a man of deep faith, Noel. Go and treat them in keeping with your beliefs. Then come over to the Chambers and we'll celebrate with coffee and cakes.'

We were faced with a barrage of reporters and microphones. I'd arranged with Bob that he'd assemble the press and we'd have an orderly interview. He was nowhere to be seen!

'No comment at the moment. I'll answer your questions as soon as Bob Westerdale arrives.'

We walked down the corridor, the press hot on our heels. Bob was apparently on the phone filing his story before the others did. Typical journalist! We stopped and managed to bring a degree of order. About twenty minutes later they were happy.

We were stopped by a representative from ITN television and we arranged to do an interview. Then police officers Allan Potts and Eric Evans came up and congratulated me. I thanked them both for all their dedicated work and effort.

In Chambers we found both Ian Hughes and the Crown representative, Mr Clegg. It was strange celebrating our victory with both sets of counsel.

'It's good to have a case you really believe in,' said Mr Clegg.

I wondered how many cases go before the courts that counsel doesn't believe in.

After the TV interview we headed for home. The journey back was so different from the one that morning. We were jubilant. I kept cheering, shaking my fists in the air.

'I'm free! I'm free!'

Nearer home Keith asked me, 'What'll you do with all the begging letters?'

I thought for a second. 'I intend to keep sending them!'

The whole car rocked to laughter.

We arrived home to the sound of the telephone ringing. It was the first of hundreds of well-wishers who kept the line busy for much of that week. Then, before Coral could make us a cup of tea, a TV crew from the BBC turned up.

'Oh, no, I don't think I can handle any more media right now,' I said.

'Listen, mate,' said Bob. 'It's been a big day. Let the world know what it's like to be vindicated. You might as well get it over with now. Then they'll leave you in peace.'

I hadn't really imagined the impact of this final

day in my struggle for justice. All this attention had taken me by surprise.

Within the hour the TV crew had left and all three of our girls arrived home. The lounge was awash with tears of joy as we hugged each other and sobbed in unison.

'It's finally over. Isn't God good?' I said.

No one really answered. They just hugged me and shed more tears of love and joy on my behalf. It was a precious moment for me as all I'd given them in the past was returned to me in their reaction to my news.

In between taking turns answering the phone, I decided we'd have fish and chips from the takeaway to celebrate. But Coral and the girls wanted the full treatment in a restaurant.

Before going out, we watched both ITV and BBC TV news, cheering wildly as the two stations ran the full interviews and gave background information about the case. That morning we'd been unknown people; now, on the biggest day of our lives, we were being screened to millions of people.

Following the news reports I sat thinking how incredible the support and media coverage was. Where were they all in 1970 when I really needed them?

We found a quiet restaurant and celebrated with a fine meal. But soon the girls wanted to get home for the next news broadcasts so they could video them. I didn't put up much of a fight.

We spent the rest of the evening watching news bulletins and cracking open the bottles of champagne Bob and I had bought for the occasion.

Shortly after midnight, tiredness overtook me. I wanted to fight it—I didn't want the day to end in case I woke up and it had all been a dream.

What a remarkable day it had been! I'd been vindicated, God had been glorified and I could look forward to living in that certain truth.

I woke at 6.45, dropped Bob off at the station and bought every national newspaper. All of them had covered the story comprehensively. So it really was true.

Leaning over the breakfast bar reading about myself, I remembered the words of a man I'd admired ever since I'd read his speeches while in Wakefield prison.

Martin Luther King had said in his Nobel peace prize speech, 'Free at last. Free at last. Lord God Almighty, I'm free at last.'

I now understood the full meaning of those words. They echoed Jesus' words: 'If the Son makes you free, you shall be free indeed.'

What more could any person ask? Now I had it all—freedom of thought, speech, choice and movement.

18 On the Road

Following my vindication I was inundated by offers and requests to write a book, detailing all my experiences. The proposals were obviously flattering, but I wasn't sure if I could handle all the publicity and exposure my story would inevitably bring to myself and my family. Having discussed it at great length with Coral, and considered all the offers, I decided to sign for Lion Publishing. They talked about ghostwriters and my ability to write the book. After several discussions with Lion, I agreed to have a go. In truth I knew that no one else could realistically tell my story, projecting all those emotions and experiences on to the printed page. With some feelings of trepidation I turned reams of snow-white paper into a pilot for *Killing Time*. Lion appeared excited at the style and content I'd put together and agreed I was to be the author of my own story.

I set myself a target of writing a minimum of a thousand words per day, and because of my work commitments, this began in the evening. I also tried to compose two thousand words per day over the weekend. This proved to be very hard work, both mentally and emotionally, as the full story started to pour out from my pen. I had already booked a holiday for myself, Coral and Olivia, at the end of August, at the Grand Tinerfe Hotel on the island of Tenerife. After great persuasion on my behalf, Coral agreed that I could continue to write on holiday, albeit between 8a.m. and noon. This would enable me to keep the continuity of writing up and fulfil my contract with Lion. Following lunch, every day, I would spend the afternoon with Coral and Olivia, lounging around the pool, sunbathing and generally relaxing.

On one such afternoon I found myself in conversation with a man called Graham Nethercot. We were idly passing the time of day when I noticed Graham reading a paperback and asked him what made him buy it. He thought it a strange question and asked me the reason behind the request. I informed him that I was writing a book and was interested in what motivated people to choose a particular book. For a couple of hours I proceeded to tell him my life story and it was plain to see he was absolutely amazed at what he was hearing.

Graham wanted to continue our conversation at dinner and invited Coral and me to meet his wife, Gail, at the pool-side bar. Later on, as Graham left for the dining-room, it was obvious he was struggling to walk properly. I had in fact observed him for some time, and noticed that he never entered the swimming pool and was always seen under the shade of a tree, reading a book. Thinking little of our companion's unsteady gait, we all followed him to dinner. Following the meal we all sat under a Spanish night full of stars and passed the usual pleasantries, then Graham was back to asking about all the injustice I had suffered.

At some point I mentioned to him that I had noticed him hobbling to get from one point to another. Apparently, Graham had suffered from an acute back problem for a number of years and had seen every disc specialist possible. They had all given him the same diagnosis: there was nothing they could do for such a condition. Graham was a top executive who earned a tremendous salary, and had even paid privately, to no avail, a Harley Street surgeon.

Somewhat spontaneously I said to Graham, 'I know a man that can heal you.'

He laughed at my comment and said, 'I've already told you, I've seen every specialist in the country. They all came up with the same diagnosis, there's nothing anybody can do about my condition.'

I tried again, 'But I know a man that *can* heal you.'

Graham said, 'Well, where is he?'

'Right here in Tenerife.' I replied.

Graham asked me where he was staying.

'Right here in the Grand Tinerfe Hotel!' I said sipping my drink.

Graham asked his name.

'His name is Jesus.' I smiled confidently.

With that Graham and his wife, Gail, burst out laughing. I felt somewhat uncomfortable, but did not back off from what I knew to be true. I reminded the couple of everything that had happened to me and all the healing that had already taken place in my life, physically and emotionally.

I said to Graham, 'You may not know Jesus as I know him, you may not have the faith that I have, but if you will just let me pray for you, I really believe that God can heal you.'

Graham and Gail suddenly became serious.

'What have you got to lose?' I asked, looking for any signs of hope.

'OK, what do you want me to do?' Graham said, a slight flutter in his voice.

I told him to lean forward. I placed my hands on his back and I prayed, asking God to stretch forth his hand of healing and to restore Graham's back to wholeness. I sensed tremendous heat pouring from his back and felt sure that God was healing him. God did! Shortly afterwards we all went for a stroll together and Graham walked the furthest he had walked for years, with no back pain. The distance we covered was close on three miles.

The next day, as I emerged from my balcony, having finished writing for the day, I saw Graham thrashing about in the pool with Olivia. Gail, who was at the side of the pool, looked on anxiously and excitedly. Interestingly enough, Coral had woken that morning and felt a need to pray about Gail; she sensed Gail seemed to have a fear of water.

Coral felt God was telling her it was something to do with Gail's father. As we were chatting in the afternoon, Coral bought the subject up and explained what she had experienced that morning. Gail appeared completely shocked, and in fact one could physically see the blood drain from her face. Once she had gathered herself together, she told us that her father had been killed in the war; he'd actually drowned. Coral explained to Gail that if God had revealed something to her that she had no foreknowledge about, then she believed that he could remove this controlling fear. Gail would then be able to enjoy the water like everyone else.

So here we were again, praying for Gail this time, by the pool-side. Yet again, God set another captive free! Later that day, Coral took Gail into the swimming pool for the first time in her life and started to teach her to swim.

What astounded me more than anything else was that these two people hadn't professed a personal relationship with Jesus Christ, hadn't professed to be Christians, but still, God in his love and grace had spectacularly set them free. There I was, supposed to be on holiday, writing a book and finding myself involved in the most bizarre happenings. How could two people experience the power of God's healing upon their lives and circumstances, yet leave Tenerife non-Christians? None of it made any sense. However, a small seed had been sown that would later bear fruit.

It was never my intention to go out and speak publicly about my life. After all I had no experience in it, I had no training in public speaking and, more importantly, it wasn't something I really wanted to do. However, things don't always work out the way you think they will. Graham Hughes, my solicitor, had asked me to speak at a Full Gospel Businessmen's dinner, on the Isle of Wight. Like a fool I agreed to do it, without considering the consequence of such a decision. I found myself trying to finish the book and also concoct a speech for the meeting on the Isle of Wight. I spent seven nights trying to put together an address that would adequately cover all the points of my experience—within forty minutes. Bins full of waste paper later I finally completed the speech.

We were due to go to the Isle of Wight in late October 1986. Graham had told me that because the holiday season was over, there was no need to book the ferry for the car, as we would easily roll on and roll off. The morning arrived and I, Coral and Olivia, packed the car and headed down to Portsmouth to catch the ferry.

After a short while Coral looked across at me and said, 'Noel, you've forgotten your cigarettes.'

'No, I haven't,' I offered without looking.

'Well, I can't see them in the car.'

I explained to Coral that I had been praying to God about my smoking. 'I told him I enjoyed a cigarette,' which I had done for many years, 'and I had no real desire to give up. But if God was calling me into the public domain as far as speaking or ministry work was concerned, I wanted him to remove the longing to smoke.' At that time I was probably smoking thirty cigarettes a day and had done for a long time, even after becoming a Christian. It never ceased to amaze me, the number of Christians who, over the years, had said to me, 'Do you smoke?' 'Yes,' I would always reply. One could sense their judgment and disgust at my apparent addiction.

Disappointment is very often born out of expectancy. Christians very often expect too much of people who come into the 'family of believers' and don't change their life's habits and addictions over night. It reminds me of the bishop who was not convinced that a convicted murderer had really become a Christian. The chaplain took the bishop into prison to meet the inmate. After a somewhat lengthy interview the bishop concluded that the prisoner had unquestionably committed his life to Christ.

'Chaplain, what you need to do is get this man to stop smoking,' requested the bishop.

The chaplain replied, 'Don't you think it would be a good idea to get him to stop killing people first?'

I said to Coral that I had spoken to God and told him that if he wanted me to speak publicly, then he would have to remove the desire for me to smoke. I concluded by saying, 'From today I am a non-smoker.' Coral looked at Olivia, Olivia looked at Coral. Their eyes said it all—'It's going to be a very interesting trip!'

We arrived at Portsmouth to find the ferry was booked solid, and the next one, and the next one. I entered the early stages of nicotine withdrawal and became more and more agitated as time went slowly by. Eventually we embarked on the ferry in the middle of the afternoon. I found myself pacing up and down the walkway, drinking tea, eating cakes, eating crisps, just eating, eating, eating. It was all a brave fight against the ravages of the noxious weed. It seemed everywhere I looked, on the ferry, people were smoking. I even tried to sniff in the smoke through my nostrils, searching for the calming effect of the nicotine. In my own heart I knew the battle was on.

We all arrived at the Isle of Wight, began to disembark, and found ourselves behind a large juggernaut lorry, which broke down on the ramp going off the ferry. I just couldn't believe what was happening to us. I reached a point where I would do anything for a cigarette. That small, white filtered tube was the answer to all my problems. By the time the lorry was removed it was close to 5p.m. We headed towards our destination. After only one mile down the road we found ourselves in the middle of a gigantic traffic jam—on the Isle of Wight, in *October*! Now I was willing to kill someone for a cigarette. As we slowly merged into the traffic and stopped, I glanced up at a large advertising hoarding. It was for Rothmans! The very brand of cigarette I had smoked for years.

'That's a sign from God,' I said to Coral. 'He's telling me to buy some Rothmans.'

She simply said, 'That's the devil overplaying his hand.' Eventually I came round to her way of thinking.

We reached our host's house fifteen minutes before the dinner was to begin. I literally had a quick wash, changed and headed for the meeting. The withdrawal symptoms had now consumed my every thought. I felt light headed and my body was shaking. I survived the meal and then, without prior warning, I was suddenly introduced to a couple of hundred people. Instant flashback of coming out of Wakefield Prison, that cold January morning, with no future expectation of a quality of life whatsoever, yet here I was, standing ready to speak to hundreds of people.

I remember thinking, 'What on earth are you doing, Noel?' I had spent the last seven years attending a church, but had never spoken publicly at all. Surely the best way would have been to start with a smaller group. I reached inside my jacket for the speech I had spent seven days preparing. Utter horror, it wasn't there! The numbing shock of the reality of what I had done suddenly sunk in. I had left my neatly folded speech on the dressing table at home. I stood there, rooted to the spot, shaking like a rag doll and my mouth bone dry.

After what seemed like an eternity, I whispered to God, 'God, you and I are in trouble. If you don't fill my mouth with words, public speaking for me finishes at this point.' With that I opened my mouth and said, 'Ladies and gentlemen, it is a great pleasure to be here with you tonight.' All the nervousness ceased, confidence came and everything I'd written came to memory. I spoke for the next forty-five minutes.

I concluded with a challenge to the audience. If they wanted what I had got in a personal relationship with Jesus Christ they could have it right there and then. All they needed to do was to meet the conditions that I had outlined, and accept Jesus Christ as their Lord and saviour. I told them that if anyone wanted to make that commitment tonight they should stand. I couldn't believe what I had just said. And yet within seconds, all over the room, people started to stand. There must have been thirty to forty people standing. For me that was a sign that God had a far bigger plan for my life than I could have ever imagined. Perhaps even more significantly, God removed my desire to smoke.

That was the start of a long journey on the road that, over the next few years, took me all over the country. I visited churches, schools, colleges, universities; the demand became greater and greater. The book was launched in another great wave of national publicity, which again opened many avenues of opportunity to speak more frequently to people. The great difficulty was that people looked at me as someone who had something more than they had. All I had was exactly what they had: the Lord Jesus Christ. It was the same Jesus with the same promise. I simply believed the Bible and God's promises; I preached the gospel and prayed for the sick. People turned to God, people were healed and people were set free. It was nothing to do with me, but everything to do with God. I really resented being placed on a pedestal. I was only Noel Fellowes, another sinner who'd been forgiven by God, wanting to give away what had been given to me, so that others might know the freedom and healing that I'd experienced in my own life.

It's one thing to have a reputation, it's another thing to have the truth. One of the problems I faced with reputation was that some Christians became disappointed in me. As people came forward to pray, some walked away healed, others walked away the same way they came. And to this day I don't know who was cured and who remained the same.

There were certainly some significant healings that spring to mind.

I was speaking at a large church in the Midlands, mainly telling my story, and at the end of the meeting I made an appeal to those who wanted to make a commitment to Jesus. I also asked for anyone who was sick to come forward and we would pray for them. In the middle of making this request I noticed the minister of the church looking nervous and edgy. As all the people stood up and started coming forward, he rose to his feet and headed for the vestry. The aisles were full with people wanting to be prayed for. I looked at Coral, she looked at me. Betty and Keith, our friends who were with us, also exchanged glances.

I said, 'Would the elders and the leaders of the church please come forward and start ministering to these people.' No one moved. At that point I knew we were in deep trouble. Someone whispered in my ear, 'The elders and the leaders are all standing with everybody else in the aisles.'

So there we were, Coral, myself, Keith and Betty, praying for all these people, one by one. Two hours or so later we had finished. Just as we were about to leave, the vestry door opened and out walked the minister, looking anxious and shaken. His concern was that no one normally made appeals in his church and he was convinced that the elders or the leaders would want to discipline him for allowing such a thing to happen. When I explained to him that his elders and leaders were all queuing up to be prayed for, his whole countenance changed and one could see the man had been deeply touched. Six months later I was invited back. It was unrecognizable as the church I had once visited. Gone was the dead tradition, gone was the rigid formality of worship; the place was really alive and people were truly free.

Before I was about to preach I sensed God give me a 'word of knowledge' to tell to a woman in the meeting who'd been systematically raped and had been traumatised by the whole experience. I took a large gulp and delivered God's message. You could have heard a pin drop. Suddenly, the woman in question screamed out. I was as shocked as everyone else at the meeting; I really didn't have a clue what I should do. I was praying in my head all the time, 'What shall I do, Lord, what shall I do?' I sensed God telling me to start praying over this woman. I left the platform and walked to where she was, crying out in hysterics. I raised my hands above the woman and began to pray for her. Suddenly she stopped screaming, fell to the floor and just lay there as if in a deep sleep. I returned to the platform and resumed preaching. At the end of the meeting she was still lying on the floor, with those around her quite concerned about what they should do. I sensed God saying, 'Just leave her.' I knew that if God was in control of the situation, he was dealing with all the issues of trauma and pain that she had gone through. She was still lying there when we came back for the evening meeting.

What I learned about this woman over lunch was the most horrifying story I had ever heard. The minister had told me that no one else in the church had known about her story. She had in fact been a missionary in Africa. She had been kidnapped by some tribesmen, along with a couple of other women, and had been systematically raped by these men for six days. The missionary society had flown her back to England and asked the minister to arrange treatment and counselling. He had taken her into his home and he and his wife took it in turns, every night, just sitting in her bedroom with the light on, playing Christian music, because her nightmares were so intense. They had actually been doing that for the last three weeks and had seen little change in her nightly pattern.

Some way into the evening meeting the woman started to groan then suddenly rose to her feet. She was unrecognizable as the woman I had seen in the morning. A gentle smile played around her face and she had peace in her eyes. She told us that she had been in Jesus' presence. And that was all she could remember. She had been under the master surgeon's knife, been operated upon, supernaturally healed with no apparent scar tissue. Six months later the same woman wrote to us: she was back in the mission field of Africa.

In contrast to churches, I also find myself being invited to speak in more prison settings. The last thing I ever wanted to do was to go back into prison. And yet it was in prisons that I felt the most freedom; it seemed far easier to speak to people who truly understood where I had come from. Prisoners understood the issues—I had been an ex-policeman and I had been an innocent man in prison. Those two reasons were enough for all the prisoners to come forward and listen.

One meeting that sticks out in my memory was at Strangeways, before it was burnt down. The chaplain was a man called Noel Procter. He was a real zealot for God, respected throughout the country by both prison officers and inmates. He invited me to go and speak. I arrived in the chapel, which had tiered seating like a theatre, and held about five hundred men. The place was packed, there wasn't a seat empty. I took a friend of mine, Sid Stevens, with me, who had never been inside a prison before. He suddenly found himself inside Strangeways prison, facing five hundred inmates, who were shouting, whistling and generally giving Noel Procter a hard time. I looked across at Sid and could see every muscle in his body shake from head to toe, his suit was actually moving.

After the chaplain's opening address he intro-duced me to speak, '... I have a man here today; his name is Noel Fellowes, an ex-policeman...' As soon as he uttered the word 'policeman' the whole place erupted. Inmates started bawling, swearing and throwing things. The noise was deafening. Again I glanced over at Sid. Now he wasn't just shaking, he'd gone ashen white.

I strolled up to the podium, slightly nervous myself, and shouted at the top of my voice. 'I know what it's like to be banged up in a prison. I also know that the person prisoners trust the most inside is the prison chaplain. He's the one who helps you with your marriage problems and he's the one who gets you special visits for wives and families.' The place got quieter and quieter. I continued, 'The only person who respects you in *this* prison is this man, Noel Procter. When he walks into your cell, he respects you as a person. Not as a number, not as a convict, but as a person. Well, now you're in *his* cell. His cell is called this church. So I'm asking *you* to respect Noel Procter's cell. So shut up and listen.' The battle had been won. Everybody just went silent. For the next forty-five minutes I simply told my story.

I concluded by saying, 'The evidence demands a verdict. Any man who wants to know freedom today, can. Just leave your name with one of the orderlies as you leave the chapel building. Noel and his team will definitely come to see you today or tomorrow.' Over forty men left their names. They all wanted to make a decision for Jesus Christ; they were willing to try and turn their lives round and make a fresh start. The numbers increased as the week went on. Noel wrote and told me about the impact that morning service had on so many more lives. The irony is, I never took Sid into another prison.

Having spoken in a church on the edge of South London and made an appeal for people to come forward for salvation and healing, in the prayer line I spotted a woman in her late twenties in a wheelchair. She informed me that she had been struck down by some crippling disease, some years ago and that she was now an invalid and prisoner to the chair. She lived in a bungalow with ramps and all the necessary fitments and accessories needed for a disabled person.

What struck me about this young woman was her love for Jesus and her faith that God would heal her. I had reached the conclusion, a long time ago, that it was no-thing to do with me, it was all to do with God, so I never found it difficult to pray for anyone. I took her hand in my hands and started to pray that God would heal, uplift and restore this woman to the perfection of his creation.

I continued to pray and pray and, slowly but surely, she started to get up out of the wheelchair. People were shouting and clapping. My instant thought was, 'She probably never needed to be in a wheelchair. This is not really a big deal.' Then I saw the tears pouring down her face. Through her tears she thanked God over and over again. At that point I *knew* it was real.

With that I said to her, 'Is there anything else? I just sense there's something else you want God to do for you.' She told me about her particular condition, which meant she could never have children. A verse of scripture came to mind: Psalm 37 verse 4.

I began, 'Those who delight in the Lord, he will give them their heart's desire.' She confirmed her heart's desire was to have a child. I simply prayed that God would grant her heart's desire. With that I left, absolutely astounded at what God had done for her that night. The following day, which was a Sunday, I received a call from the vicar of a church she attended. I had thought she attended the church I had spoken at that night, but she actually belonged to an Anglican church a few miles down the road. The vicar went on to explain to me that this lady had been confined to a wheelchair for six years and had walked into the church on Sunday morning. Everybody had been truly amazed and astonished at God's healing of her. Any doubts I'd had were suddenly dispelled. It was an incredible privilege to see such a healing take place.

A few months later I received a letter from her, which explained to me how much her healing had cost her. She had had to come off invalidity benefit and give up her bungalow, together with all her special fitments. As she had now been cured, her safety net had been removed and now she faced a life and a future. More importantly she told me that the doctors couldn't believe it, but she was three months pregnant.

I received a letter when the baby was born. How truly incredible God is.

Speaking in a city mission, in the heart of London one night, I arrived at the meeting hall and found a fleet of ambulances outside. They were wheeling all sorts of people into the meeting. Rather confused I asked someone if this was the correct building for the Christian service. The person informed me I was in exactly the right place. The hall was packed with people and still people were being shown in. The funny part was that all the street people came in and sat on the platform, which was the only space available. As I stood up to speak, many of them weren't sitting any more; they were just lying down, fast asleep.

There I was speaking at the podium, with a platform full of drunken men. The smell of their clothes, bodies and alcohol invaded every breath. A number of them then had the audacity to start snoring while I was in mid-flow! As I was speaking, I was trying to turn them over, so they would stop snoring and everybody else could hear me. It turned out to be a very strange experience indeed.

To some degree life is like that, we are never prepared for the sudden twist of destiny. One minute, or even one second everything can be absolutely wonderful and the next moment disaster can strike without any warning whatsoever.

I spoke at a meeting in London, with Coral, Olivia, my brother John and his wife, Gill, and their two sons. We enjoyed a great evening of celebration together. It was one of those very special occasions where people responded to God. Everyone showed great expectancy and a level of faith that was almost touchable. People were healed and people were set free.

We returned home around midnight, still on a tremendous high. As I entered the front door the telephone was ringing. I picked up the phone and heard my mother's voice. She sounded very shaky and distressed. She asked me to come over to her home as Dad looked very ill. I said I would be right over in five minutes.

Deep down in my heart I knew there was something seriously wrong. My mother isn't the sort of person who panics or asks anybody for help, without good cause. I arrived at my parents' home and saw my mother standing on the front step looking very shaken.

I rushed over to the house with my mother's words echoing in my ears, 'It's your dad, it's your dad. I think he's having an attack.'

I went straight into the bedroom and saw my father lying in bed, slightly propped up with pillows. He was staring into space with a glazed look in his eyes. His posture seemed awkward. I wrapped my arms around his chest to try and help him to a more comfortable position. I heard him exhale, a deep sigh. At that moment I knew he was dead.

I had seen the death mask many times before, when I was in the police force dealing with sudden deaths. The strange thing was, I couldn't come to terms with the fact that my father had died. Anger seemed to rise from nowhere. I felt utterly and completely robbed. I gazed upon my father's face and thought, 'I never knew this man. Now I will never know him. This is my father.'

The next thing I remember was an audible voice saying, 'I've taken him home, Noel.' I searched the dimly lit bedroom to see if anyone was there. My mother was standing right behind me.

'The Lord's just told me, Mum; he's taking Dad home.'

My mother replied, 'That's right, son, that's right. I heard it too.'

I glanced around the bedroom and saw my father's trousers hanging over the end of the bed. His other clothes were neatly folded on a chair. Obviously he had expected to get up in the morning to face the challenge of a new day. I just couldn't come to terms with what had happened. How was it that only a couple of hours before I was in the middle of a meeting, seeing all these wonderful things happening and here I was kneeling at my dead father's bedside.

Feelings of betrayal surrounding my younger years and painful memories flooded back of a childhood that was speckled with misunderstandings and hurt. Father and I never really hit it off or even got on in our lives. My mother had prayed for my father non-stop, for thirty-seven years, that he would come to know God. When I became a Christian, I immediately went round to my parents and told them of my experiences.

I can remember my father saying to my mother, 'If *he's* found God, there must be one.' The very next day he became a Christian. That had really been the start of our relationship. There were so many things that had never been said, so many issues that had never been resolved; we were just working through them one by one, trying to build something that would truly reflect our new-found beliefs. His early death had left a huge hole in my life.

My mother and I knelt and prayed, thanking God for my father's life. We also thanked God that he was now in God's care in his eternal kingdom. That was the only comforting truth in this whole traumatic experience.

I don't know how long we prayed, before I rang to tell my brothers, Roger, John and Paul. One by one they turned up, all trying to handle their sorrow and grief in their own particular way. I looked up and saw the family all kneeling in prayer.

'Perhaps we should ring a doctor?' I said. It sounded ironic. It was obvious my father was dead; the first stages of rigor mortis had taken place.

The doctor who arrived turned out to be a locum. I explained the circumstances and the time delay. I told him we'd simply been praying.

To my amazement, he said, 'I'm a Christian. Would you mind if I prayed with you?' So there we all were praying together. We were there all night.

As dawn broke, I realized with surprise that a new day was beginning. Night had gone and the day had come, a new day and a new chapter in my own distinctive book of life.

Death has a way of bringing life back into perspective. It was time to reevaluate all I was doing and what I was planning for the future.

On a number of occasions I had sensed that God was calling me into full-time Christian ministry. Yet I enjoyed the dual role I had in life; working in the day, earning money through the business that inevitably helped to fund my work for God. It gave me great freedom. I didn't have to concern myself about travelling expenses or be restricted by churches that were financially embarrassed. I was free to travel anywhere.

Danielle was now married, Louise had qualified as a midwife and Olivia was preparing for Manchester University, studying art and design. I still had a financial responsibility to them to fulfil and didn't want my family to sacrifice their careers and their future for the sake of my desire to go full-time into Christian ministry. It was also a great privilege to travel throughout the country across all denominational boundaries.

I remember lying in bed one night thinking, 'As a Christian I have probably seen more in a few years on the road than most Christians could see in their whole lifetime. If it was all to stop tomorrow morning I could have no complaints, because it had been such a wonderful privilege. I have seen the sick healed, the broken restored, the rejected finding worth and value and the lost finding purpose and truth, documented in the hundreds and hundreds of letters that had been written to us over the years—living proof that God is still in the restoring business.'

19 Call Versus Choice

The end of the eighties saw a massive depression in the construction industry and work became very scarce. I had ridden the storm, as the majority of my business was industrial maintenance with a large company in Bracknell called British Aerospace. Then out of the blue came the news that the Bracknell operation was to close down and be transferred to Plymouth. What had become a secure financial brace for my business was now being removed in the next three months. It was one of those inevitable times when I had to first examine where my security lay. Was it in the comfort of sustained financial assurance, or in my faith that God would see us through?

The truth is, God is wonderful when things are going well and it's very easy to praise and worship Him. The rubber hits the road when times are hard; that's when your conviction to God is tested. It was obvious to me that the sudden shutdown of British Aerospace, and the huge recession, meant that only the strongest and fittest outfits would survive. It also became clear that there were many builders who were simply pricing jobs to cover their overheads, with no built-in profit margin, literally to endure the storm.

While all of this was taking place, I faced another uphill battle. Violence in prison had caught up with me, over the years, as discs in both my neck and lower back became ever more painful. My friend and doctor, Maurice Robinson, who was also an elder in the church, suggested I had a series of X-rays to view the amount of damage. The results were quite devastating.

I sat in Maurice's surgery and he simply said, 'Noel, if I didn't know you from the man you are today and all I had were these X-rays, due to the damage and wear I'd have thought they belonged to a man in his late seventies.'

Ironically, that news came only four or five weeks before we were due to go skiing in France. I told Maurice of our proposed holiday over Christmas. He said, in no uncertain terms, that I wasn't even to *put on* a pair of skis. He did all he could to stop me from making the trip, or at least from skiing. I suspect deep down in his heart he knew what I would do. No matter what the odds, I have always been a fighter and have never surrendered to the possibility of defeat.

Christmas came and off we went to enjoy our first skiing holiday. No sooner had we arrived than

Danielle, her husband Kevin and Olivia were straight out on their skis. The overnight train journey and subsequent coach travel had left me feeling quite sore and stiff. So I decided to rest and join a class on the second day.

We were all assessed as to our balance and our capability of standing on skis. I was asked to join a beginners' group, consisting of people who had a similar skill-base to mine. I survived the first practice day, but on the second, disaster struck! The instructor had told us to follow him down a rather long ski run. Gaining confidence in my skiing prowess, I followed with speed and enthusiasm. However, I hadn't quite mastered the slowing-down technique and knew I was in trouble as I sailed past the instructor. In the distance I could see a large hump, and instantly decided to try and jump it. But what I thought was a large hump turned out to be the end of the ski run. I couldn't stop and took off as I hit the mound. I flew through the cold air, thinking to myself, 'I've definitely got problems here.' What seemed like an eternity in the air ended, as I knew it would, and I came back to earth with a loud thud. The impact was so great I was winded and struggling for breath.

My first thought was, 'Is anything broken?' I managed to move my head—that was all right—my arms could move and I had feeling in my hands. Then I realized that the pain in my back had gone. It was at that point I thought I was in serious trouble. There was no apparent feeling in my lower back and down through my legs. Surely the worst hadn't happened, that I was crippled for life? Then I felt sensation in my left leg and I breathed a huge sigh of relief.

I was rescued, examined and, in my inevitable way, dismissed the medics and crawled back to our apartment. The rest of the Christmas period was spent lying on my back, simply drinking alcohol to try and numb the pain.

I felt guilty because I hadn't told Coral of the continuing lack of feeling in my right leg, evidenced as I went to the toilet. I knew when I needed to go, but I never knew if I'd been or even finished. Now I believed it was time to be worried!

Within days I was back home, in hospital and having tests and X-rays. I had damaged the nerves in the base of my spine, the discs had fragmented and I needed an immediate operation. The discs had to be removed.

Everything, it seemed, had crashed around me within the last month; the business, my health and now an operation which would demand a lengthy recovery period. Nothing made sense anymore. I remember speaking out, after being in theatre, and saying to God, 'Where are you in all of this? You're supposed to be on my side.' All the memories came flooding back: the meetings, the healings, the hype and the joy. All of it was true, all of it was real—and here I was lying in a hospital bed having had a major back operation. I felt an absolute failure. How on earth could I go out again and preach healing, or lay my hands on the sick? It just didn't seem fair at all.

I went into a deep depression that no one could draw me out of. It seemed that I had to take a look at my life through a new lens and decide what I really believed in. In hindsight the reality was that God had put me back into the fire. Very often when we feel we have arrived, it's at that point God takes us back into the flames. No one could reach me, no one could talk to me and no one could help me. I had to find myself and come to terms with the fact that all my willpower and all my strength couldn't lift me out of the pit I found myself in. In the months that lay ahead I once again unwrapped my life and asked God to operate in the areas that needed deep surgery.

Ten months later I woke up one morning and felt better. I understood the road that God wanted me to take. For years I'd chosen to do the things I wanted to do, I had chosen to go where I wanted to go. I had chosen to speak where I wanted to speak and I had chosen the platforms I wanted to stand on. On that day I knew that God had called me into full-time ministry. Irresistibly it was call versus choice, but where would I start? I had responsibilities. I needed a job and I needed money. I had closed the business down nearly a year ago and had used all our savings to fund us through the months of hardship.

Within the first week I'd received two phone calls, both asking me if I would consider being interviewed for vacancies in their respective organizations. The first call was from Peter Chadwick, the Executive Director of Prison Fellowship,

England and Wales, a national Christian organization which works alongside prisoners, ex-prisoners and their families. I had met Peter a number of years before and had been an avid supporter of the Prison Fellowship. He told me they needed to move on in all areas of the ministry, particularly in attracting more core funding. Any financial gain could also fund future projects. The last thing I ever wanted to do was to work full-time in prison ministry, but I decided to visit Peter and discuss it.

The second call I received was from a management training organization. They'd heard through the grapevine that I was available for work. I went for the interview and felt excited at the prospect of leading modular management training seminars, especially as their clients included BMW and the Ford Motor Company.

I went back for a second interview and was offered a position which included a package of £35,000 per annum, plus expenses, plus a 7 series BMW. It all seemed too good to be true. There was no question in my mind, I definitely wanted to do this job.

I arrived home to a message from Peter Chadwick. He wanted me to join them at Prison Fellowship. Peter informed me that he'd met with the trustees and they'd decided to offer me the position of Development Director, on a yearly salary of £10,000, plus a mileage allowance. I spent a sleepless night tossing and turning, wanting to make the right decision, but knowing deep down I wanted to do God's work.

The next day I telephoned Peter Chadwick and told him I would take the position offered. I spoke to the other company, informing them of my decision not to join them and telling them of my deep conviction that I should work with Prison Fellowship. They responded magnificently by offering me £200 per day, with expenses, if I would consider doing selective seminars for them. I toyed with the idea, but came to the conclusion that if I was to be committed to the *call*, then nothing else should deflect me.

I got stuck into the challenge and the work of Prison Fellowship. The first obstacle to overcome was fitting into a team. I had come from a different environment, working on my own initiative for the last ten years, but I knuckled down and overcame the hurdles. Within a matter of months I felt established, accepted and motivated by not only the quality of the team but the commitment people had to the ministry. On the down side, funding was a major problem and every day we'd pray and pray for money that would pay the everyday expenses. I remember coming home, following the first month, and saying to Coral, 'I really enjoyed the work, but unfortunately there wasn't enough money to pay my salary.'

Coral looked at me and said, 'Noel, are you sure you've made the right decision? Did God really call you to this work?'

Deep down in my heart I knew this was the place for me and that somehow God would pay our mortgage, pay our bills and provide for our every need. How we survived I honestly don't know, but every month we had more money than bills. Somehow everything seemed to get paid. Money arrived in all sorts of different packages, very often from people we'd never known or even met. It was increasingly difficult for me to accept such gifts as I'd always found pleasure in giving. It seemed so strange to think that not long ago I had a business that made enough money to keep us at a comfortable standard of living. I had never needed to ask for anything but here I was in the position where we were all living off other people's generosity—it was just so humbling. It took time to sink in, but I realized that God was teaching me, in his own inimitable way, how to receive.

Financial strain did not ease with the continuation of Prison Fellowship. I soon came to the conclusion that whatever ministry you were involved in, there was never going to be enough money to support the work that needed to be done. This need kept me focused, as well as testing all the staff to the limits with problems; week in, week out, month in, month out. In retrospect, God certainly made our dreams come true and maintained our impetus to carry on. It appeared at the time that God was never late; the trouble is, when you're in the middle of a particular difficulty, it seems as though he's never early! As time passed I learnt not to rely on my own understanding, but to trust in God for the future of the work.

A year or so after joining Prison Fellowship I found myself sat across a table with an ex-gangster called Frank Costantino. Frank was from Florida and had spoken at major Christian prison projects across the USA. He provided prison chaplains with testimony books, tapes and all kinds of literature that would help bring the message of the practical good news of Jesus Christ into individual prisoners' lives. The reason behind our meeting was to try and establish a nationwide Book Ministry to serve the hundred and thirty or so prisons currently in England and Wales. Frank was looking to set up a partnership with us. He was very happy to fund it, from the American side initially, as long as the books and tapes didn't sit on dusty shelves in chaplains' offices.

This was to be the start of a wonderful adventure with a man who had incredible discernment and perception. Frank had developed Christian Prison Ministries in America and over the last twenty years had gained international recognition as one of the leading authorities on Christian work in prisons. From the first moment I spoke to Frank I knew he was a man I could learn much from; the bonus was, he was a man's man.

I was given the task of setting up and organizing the formation of Christian Prison Book Ministries. It was to run as a separate charitable trust, with Frank Costantino, myself and Captain Ian Furggerson, of the Church Army, who represented the chaplaincy. As with all things it took an awful lot of effort, not only to market the idea, but to attract the right people to fund it. Enter Graham and Gail Nethercot.

Remember, these were the people I had met in Tenerife a number of years before, who had experienced God's healing power. What had started out as a holiday friendship developed, over the years, into a benevolent attachment.

It took some years after that healing experience for Graham to become a Christian. Then Gail followed him, then their son and daughter-in-law and finally their daughter also became Christians; the whole family were baptized both in water and in the Holy Spirit. Graham, coming from a business background, gave us all the help necessary to set up the Book Ministry on a proper footing. In fact, both Graham and Gail gave up a year with no pay to raise funds, promote and administer the campaign. They set the whole thing on a firm foundation.

To date we have put over a hundred and sixty thousand Christian books into prisons all over the United Kingdom. Hundreds of letters are being received from inmates as a result of reading these life-changing books.

In my role as development director for Prison Fellowship, I travelled quite extensively in this country. As the crusade moved on I was asked to speak at different conferences and seminars all over the world. On one such trip I visited Malta for a Prison Fellowship international regional conference. One of the highlights of the conference was a banquet where the President of Malta and many top government officials were to be present. An hour before the dinner was to commence, I was informed by the International Director of Prison Fellowship that I was to give an address for twenty minutes. The bombshell had been dropped. I hadn't had a clue that I was to carry out such a prestigious honour.

The dinner over, I stood up to speak and gave a short potted history of my Christian experience. At the end of the evening I was approached by a Maltese official, who asked me if I would be prepared to go on television the next day. He felt that the people of Malta needed to hear, not only about the injustice I had suffered in my life, but also my dramatic conversion to Christ.

The next morning I was picked up by a huge black limousine. Some way down the road I asked how far it was to the television studio. I was informed by the official that we weren't filming at the studio. In fact, the President of Malta had invited us to film at his palace and I was to have breakfast with the President.

I stood at the bottom of the steps leading to the presidential palace and had another flashback to Wakefield. What was I doing at the foot of these magnificent steps? What was I doing having breakfast with the President of Malta? I entered the palace and walked into an enormous, lavishly decorated room. I ate a superb breakfast and chatted with the President and other officials. Finally I did the television interview and left the palace, still not quite believing that it had taken place.

I returned home on the Saturday, completely exhausted. I had no intention of going to my church on Sunday, because the last thing I needed was another meeting. I woke very early on Sunday morning and sensed God telling me to go to church. It was just one of those strange feelings.

I went along to our church and during the worship I sensed God prompting me to tell the congregation what had happened to me in Malta. The feeling got stronger and stronger, until finally I submitted and went to the platform. I related the story and linked it to the fact that the Apostle Paul had been shipwrecked on Malta. My life had been shipwrecked a number of years ago and God had rescued me from my disaster, just as he had rescued Paul. I went on to say that there were probably people there in the meeting that morning who felt that they were in the centre of disaster, that they had no hope and nowhere or no one to turn to. They were drowning and had no one to rescue them, but if they just reached out their hands to Jesus, then he would throw them the lifeline.

Unbeknown to me, there were a couple visiting the church who had planned to divorce. He was an ex-policeman who had left the police force because of a serious car accident. This led to depression, which led to all sorts of strains on the marriage and the couple split up. His wife's parents were Christians and had bought one of my tapes and sent it to him for Christmas. He was driving to work listening to my tape when he burst out crying and pulled in to the hard shoulder. Apparently he listened to the tape time and time again. Just before he was due to come and sign the decree nisi, he told his wife of his experience. He thought that if they could find the church in Bracknell that I had attended, then perhaps God would be able to help them.

He was telling this story to one of the members in the church, Bob, who said to him, 'Do you know who that man was who stood up and talked about the shipwreck this morning?'

He said no.

'That's Noel Fellowes,' concluded Bob.

'I don't believe you,' said the man, adamantly.

'I'm telling you, that's Noel Fellowes!'

At the end of the service Bob introduced the man to me and he related the whole story. I told him that I had obeyed God by coming to church. I finished by saying that if my words had been for no one else in the meeting that day, they were certainly for him. Minutes later he surrendered his life to Christ. Although he didn't realize it—he thought she'd just gone and left him—his wife had also responded to my words and was talking to a woman outside the meeting. She too gave her life to Jesus. The most wonderful thing was when their eyes met, as she re-entered the main auditorium, and both ran and threw their arms around each other, shouting at the top of their voices how much they loved each other. Some months later they joined the church, were baptized in water and gave the most incredible testimony to the power of God's love.

Our relationship with Frank Costantino developed more and more, and he very kindly offered us a vacation in Orlando, Florida. Having very limited funds at that time I explained to him that I doubted whether Coral and I would be able to afford the trip.

His reply was simply, 'No problem. I'll buy the tickets, you get your spending money.'

So off we went to the Sunshine State. Frank was the President of an organization called COPE, the Coalition of Prison Evangelists. He invited me to become a member of the organization and to be COPE's representative here in the United Kingdom. What you need to understand is that Frank is one of these people you don't say *no* to.

So I became the UK representative for COPE. In that role I was invited to a conference in Dallas, Texas, where I came across a couple called Charles and Sharon Burton. They headed an organization called Overcomers. For years I'd been looking for a scheme that would address all the issues I had to confront when I first became a Christian. It was true then, and it's still true today, that the church is not realistically equipped to work with some people. Multi-damaged people have special needs. Charles and Sharon had developed a twelve-step holistic programme for those suffering from serious addictions and life-controlling problems. I sat and listened and the light in my brain suddenly switched on. I knew immediately that this was the programme I'd been searching for, over many years. I asked Charles and Sharon if they would be willing to come to England, and present their material to a selected audience at our Bracknell church. They agreed.

Charles and Sharon fulfilled their promise and arrived at Bracknell. They presented their Overcomers material to a selected leadership team. Towards the end of the day, God had given me a clear vision to build a network of Overcomers groups throughout local churches and prisons in the UK. But how on earth was I ever going to start?

As always, my pastor, Ben Davies, came up trumps. He'd consistently encouraged and supported the work I was involved in and gave me the green light to pilot Overcomers at our own church: the Kerith Centre in Bracknell. There had been a number of changes to the management structure of Prison Fellowship, and I wasn't happy with the reforms that were being made and the direction the ministry was taking, so I resigned with a view to putting my efforts into the on-going Book Ministry, and implementing the vision for Overcomers within the framework of the local church and prisons throughout Britain.

For the next year I established the Overcomers programme in a number of strategic churches. I constantly evaluated the programme's content and the results of the people who had completed it, and it wasn't long before I realized this particular programme had far greater potential than its use in the USA. Primarily, it had been designed for people with drug and alcohol dependancy, but I could see that with fine-tuning the programme could help people suffering from various types of addiction or life-controlling problems.

With Charles and Sharon's permission, I rewrote

the original programme including the working manual, *A Daily Choice* and established a training package for potential group leaders. One of the rules for Overcomers is that if a person wants to be a leader, then they first have to complete the programme themselves.

To date we have four regional coordinators, and one director who runs the programme in prisons, including the training programme for leaders. The programme is based in countless churches across many denominations. It is currently being used in a number of drug and alcohol rehabilitation centres and is making an impact on many hundreds of people who suffer from addictions and life-controlling problems.

Having travelled extensively internationally, speaking in churches and conferences, my heart yearned for my own nation to be changed. There was still a piece missing. What was needed was an umbrella organization that could embrace the Book Ministry, Overcomers and Prison Ministry.

Unbeknown to me, while I was rushing around, an idea was being hatched to bring my story to the big screen. I had been approached by a number of production companies, in the UK and the States, but had never felt the time was quite right to project my experiences onto the silver screen. Time passed and I mellowed to the thought of ever doing such a thing.

I was on a ministry trip to the USA, speaking on American Christian radio and the interviewer said to me, 'Have you ever thought about making a film about *Killing Time*? Your story would make a great movie.'

I replied, 'I never really wanted *that* kind of exposure, but I suppose if the right offer came along, I would certainly consider it.' At that point I was unsure what was going to happen, but I was soon to find out.

On my return to the UK I faced the unwelcome task of opening stacks of incoming mail. Amongst the post was a letter from Bridgnorth novelist and script-writer Simon Golding, asking me if he could write a screenplay about *Killing Time*. Simon, author of *Manquito*, had heard about the book while research-ing a fictional novel at HMP Wormwood Scrubs.

There followed a telephone conversation with Simon, whose overwhelming enthusiasm shone through, persuading me to agree to let him work on a pilot script for a movie. Two months later I received a screenplay in the post. As I read the visualization, all my memories of the past came flooding back. Simon had kept very close to the book and had used some original dialogue. It all helped to paint a picture of my most darkest years.

I took Graham Nethercot with me and met Simon and his girlfriend, Amanda-Jane, at Westley Court in Kidderminster. We all chatted excitedly about the future and at the end of the meeting, I was happy to leave the project in Simon's hands. Little did I know that Hollywood was just around the corner.

I spent a great deal of time talking to Frank about my vision for the future. We both agreed it was time to launch Christian Prison Ministries in the United Kingdom. Charitable trusts were set up and in May 1995, Christian Prison Ministries was introduced to the Kerith Centre in Bracknell.

At present our government is struggling with the growing crime rate and an inability to change criminal behaviour. The church, unquestionably, is faced with the challenge and opportunity to share the life-changing message of God's love with prisoners, ex-prisoners and their families. We at Christian Prison Ministries are committed to teaching, training and supporting past and present offenders. We also hope to bring about restoration to their broken lives, through Christian training programmes such as Overcomers. Our mission is to extend our ongoing training modules into local Christian churches nationwide. It really is call versus choice, but together we can make a difference.

20 The Bigger Picture

Just when you think you have everything in order, it seems God wants you to sail the boat back into the storm. An opportunity arose to take over a large manor house, called College Hall, on the outskirts of Bracknell. It contained twenty-five rooms and was situated in extensive grounds. It was never my intention to get involved in a residential setting, as my work entailed so much time travelling, both nationally and internationally.

Once again God planted a seed of an idea in my mind. College Hall could be used to help homeless, rejected, abused and broken young adults, helping them to find truth, purpose, self-worth and fulfilment.

I prayed about the possibility of fitting College Hall into an already packed schedule, and resisted taking the project on. But as usual God had other ideas. Perfect peace is to be found when you are in the centre of God's will, I didn't have this peace without the project, and so surrendered to the inevitable thought, 'If God is in it—go for it!'

I worked throughout the Easter holidays putting together a comprehensive proposal that was to be considered by the local council and housing department. The day finally arrived and along with Ken Bothamley, one of my elders from the church, we travelled to the meeting. A thousand negative thoughts ran through my head; amongst them, had I done enough and was I prepared for their questions? Many prayers had been offered up from all our prayer partners, yet there was still a hint of apprehension in my mind. Faith is very often tinged with doubt. Doubt is very often faith in crisis.

The meeting began, and in my best possible manner I handed out the proposal documents to all present and started my presentation. I was very smooth and polished, confidently emphasising each good point.

Then I sensed God saying, 'Stop it! Stop working in your own strength and work in mine!'

Suddenly I said, 'Ladies and gentlemen, I could go on working through this proposal, but you can read it at your own leisure. I need to tell you about the vision and conviction God has given me for College Hall.'

Everyone stared at me. There was an uneasy silence and then I launched into the vision God had shown me. Twenty minutes later I had finished. The truth was I felt really good. The concept was born; it was now up to them.

Pat Munden, Chief Housing Officer, smiled at me and said, 'You really want to do this, don't you?'

'No.' I replied, 'God wants me to do it and I'm trying to be obedient to him.'

With that last comment the meeting ended. They would now discuss the scheme and let me know of their decision within the next ten days. I really had no inkling of what the outcome would be. The very next day Pat Munden telephoned to say they were very happy to run with the proposal. I couldn't believe it: the answer was yes!

We were now leasing College Hall from the council. We needed at least £40,000 per year for the rent and overheads, without even considering staff and salaries. The challenge was on, but I knew that if God was a part of it, he would provide what was needed.

Initially, there were two main supporters of the project; Bracknell Family Church and the Coign Church at Woking. The respective ministers, Ben Davies and Malcolm Kayes, pledged thousands of pounds to seed the project. Frank Costantino, in the USA, also pledged financial backing, so we signed the lease and started internal refurbishments. The twenty-five rooms, corridors and outbuildings all needed to be decorated and prepared, before occupancy could take place.

The troops rallied, volunteers came in, and local companies donated paint and equipment. Once again one could see the hand of God providing our every need. Our funds ran low extremely quickly, but still donations came pouring in: furniture, plates, kettles, right down to basic things like knives and forks—it was truly astounding. We needed to set up an administration centre that would meet the requirements of the project: in came donations of desks, chairs, computers, printers, telephones and photocopiers. All that we prayed for, all that we needed, God provided one way or another. The next requirement was to put together a team of people who had the heart and gifts to meet the needs of those who came to reside at College Hall. It was no surprise to see a team emerge who had been there, seen it, done it and bought the tee-shirt. Most had graduated through the Overcomers programme and wanted to give back what they had gained through being truly set free.

Healing is a process, not a statement. The way you handle the scars of the past will determine your future. That is what I learnt over many years as God took me apart bit by bit, and started to reshape me and remould me into the person I am today. At College Hall we don't disqualify anyone from coming into our programme of multi-tiered, multi-direction-al teaching and training, ultimately designed to prepare young adults for sustained independent living. In reality, you can only help people who want to help themselves; there must be a degree of motivation on their part.

The Bible says love overcomes all things. We don't go around striking these teenagers over the head with a hammer-shaped Bible, telling them what sinners they are—they already know that. Rather, we show them the practical good news of Jesus Christ, and try to be consistent in our love and care for them. It is not an easy path to follow, but those full of pain, hurt and rejection need to be looked after. It is out of God's love pouring through our lives that they too can come to the same knowledge of truth and salvation from Jesus Christ. It costs to care, but care we must.

We took in our first resident at the end of August, a young man who had a history of violence triggered by alcohol. Within a month I began to see a tremendous change in his attitude and behaviour. His probation officer called and asked to visit us as she had seen such a profound transformation in this young man, with whom she had been working for over a year. We didn't boast about our successes or try to impress others; we just kept to the vision and plan, letting God be God, and doing our bit for the cause.

The whole project took off from that point, resulting in senior management from probation, social services, youth justice services and other agencies visiting and referring would-be occupants to us. To date we have a host of different young adults in residence: people from care and abused backgrounds, from young offenders' institutions, those suffering from addictions, single mothers, homeless people and many others.

During this time efforts to bring *Killing Time* to the big screen were underway. It had taken several lengthy telephone calls and a few thousand miles of travel, but Simon Golding eventually secured a deal for the sale of the production rights. It was a matter of finding the appropriate production company that would give the screenplay the necessary realism and flare.

Simon, who will produce the film, held extensive talks with writer/actor Stan Foster, from Sons of Thunder Productions, California. Stan has an impressive credit list which includes a recently completed three-year overall deal at Columbia Pictures Television. He has also starred for three seasons in *Tour Of Duty*, together with many other successful productions. Stan and his partner, Lance Shultz, were very excited and motivated at the thought of making a motion picture of *Killing Time*. It was ironic that an offer should come from the States, especially as the story centred around the British judicial system. The project is planned for the '97 season and will hopefully be shown in the UK later that year.

It is a new era for me, a new challenge. It is true I never really courted publicity, and my initial feelings surrounding a movie were of suspicion, but I now sense the time is right.

Even before College Hall, I had leant that it was not easy working with people who have many different sorts of problems. However, the rewards are very satisfying when you strip away the veils of despair and find a person of worth, whom God loves, underneath. They too can become multipliers, giving away what they have experienced.

We are turning takers into givers; love only ever wants to give. For God so loved the world he gave his only-begotten son.

How much do you love humanity?
Work is love made visible.
Together we can make a difference.
Remember, one person can make a difference.
You can make a difference!

21 On Reflection

Since I went public and the case came to appeal in April 1984, many people have asked about my feelings concerning the police and the witnesses who were hostile towards me. They expect to find hatred and bitterness in my answers. But now there's no ill feeling. God has totally healed me and set me free from those negative emotions.

As a little boy in Lancashire I used to dream of what I'd do when I grew up. I wanted to be liked, secure, successful; have a loving wife and family, a nice car, a home; be my own boss; and, most of all, be happy. What I hadn't allowed for was the interim years before the dream's fulfilment.

While writing this book, I've felt detached from the person I was writing about. It seemed strange to describe yesterday's pain, suffering and injustice.

I don't really know why it all happened to me, but I believe God was in it somewhere. 'All things work together for good to those who love God,' the Bible says. It could have happened to anyone. I just hope the lessons learned will prevent it happening to someone again.

It would be easy to criticise the police over what happened, but that would be unfair to the thousands of police in the UK who've always played it by the book. I do, however, have a few words of advice for those police who were hostile towards me back in 1970: 'Sorry' is one of the most under-used words in the English vocabulary.

If I were to measure the element that most damaged me, it would be the years in prison that all but destroyed me. The main goal for a first-timer is survival in a world governed by humiliation, degradation and isolation. For most of the time inside there is little meaningful guidance for the future.

Training is given to the brighter inmate. The less fortunate semi-literate or illiterate inmate will probably leave prison the way he entered.

The Victorian buildings reflect Victorian attitudes towards their inhabitants. The inmate is trapped into being totally dependent on the system. He is told what to do and when. All a man can do is try to remain sane and survive.

In an age of changing technology, prison life remains much as it was a hundred years ago. Every long-term sentence seems coldly calculated and regulated to achieve the maximum possible humiliation.

The whole system is supervised by prison officers locking and unlocking doors, counting heads and generally being bored out of their minds. Many I met didn't enjoy the archaic system and would have preferred inmates to have more responsibility for decision-making. Unfortunately, the Home Office seems reluctant to change.

I'm not defending prisoners or criminals. If the man's guilty, then let the sentence reflect the crime. But just because some people behave like animals, is it right to treat the whole prison population as animals in cages? Having spent several years living with such people, I know that many of them deserve the chance to change and becomes assets to society again.

The alternative is frightening—anarchy, riots, untold violence and even more bitter and twisted people being returned to the outside world. Today the prison system does little more than reflect man's inhumanity to man.

Having served his sentence, an inmate goes back into society. He can pick up the threads of his past life, or he can start again from scratch. The latter was my choice, the tack I wanted to sail, leaving the past far behind. In my new life I never bargained for two visits, years later, from the police investigating killings. It's understandable that they have to interview habitual criminals, but surely not first-time offenders who've kept the slate clean and built a new life?

There's supposed to be a time limit for a person's criminal records to remain on file, but mine were still on file ten years after the offence. It would be in everyone's interests if an independent person were made responsible for destroying records correctly. If police need to interview an ex-con, I suggest more discretion and consideration. Otherwise it could destroy everything that's been achieved in a new life. Having said all that, if the vindication of the terrible injustice I suffered helps to improve the system, for me it will all have been worth it.

In telling my story I've opened the way for others to assess the merits for judicial and penal reform. For me there's another dimension—hope, forgiveness and justice from *God*.

In my long search for reality, I found no purpose, security, justice or reality in anything or anybody. Having spent years persecuting Christians and trying to disprove God's existence, I met him in a supernatural and personal way. I found reality and truth.

Since then, much has changed in my emotional, mental, physical and spiritual life. I've been healed in all those areas and become a new person. I'm not a religious freak or someone finding an escape route from the past; I'm just an ordinary, simple man who met the living God and went on to know him personally.

It'd be nice to say that since becoming a Christian everything in the garden's been rosy. But as you've already read, I've had to put my faith on the line many times. Often God seemed to be taking me apart bit by bit and rebuilding me; it was then that I felt like throwing in the towel.

Through all the peaks and troughs of my Christian experience, God has never left me. Many times he's stretched out his hand to pick me up, to strengthen me in a time of weakness and set me on the right path again.

Perfect justice, truth and reality are only to be found in Jesus Christ. God's Holy Spirit is working today through reconciliation, healing and restoring people's broken lives. How can I be sure? I've experienced this in my own life and continue to do so every day.

The best gifts in life are tied with heartstrings. I said, 'Rescue me!' And I found the love I had been looking for all of my life. Through him all things are possible.

Acknowledgments

I'd like to say a special thanks to all my family and friends who've loved and supported me through the years. To name you individually would need too long a list, but each of you knows who you are. I'm sincerely grateful for your friendship, compassion, commitment and encouragement that have sustained me through the testing years. You indeed are all part of this book.

I'd also like to extend special thanks to Bob Westerdale and his wife, Gill. Bob, who tracked me down and championed the story of my innocence in the Lancashire Evening Post, has helped make this book possible.

Many thanks to Roger Day of Life Schools Training Services, who edited the original book for distribution into prisons internationally, through Christian Prison Book Ministries.

Special thanks to Simon Golding for his work and commitment on the scriptwriting and screenplay adaptation of *Killing Time*.

Noel Fellowes

SCRIPTURA UK
(Novelist and Scriptwriter)
Simon W. Golding
1, Lonsdale Court, West Castle Street,
Bridgnorth, Shropshire,
ENGLAND
WV16 4AB